MW01093007

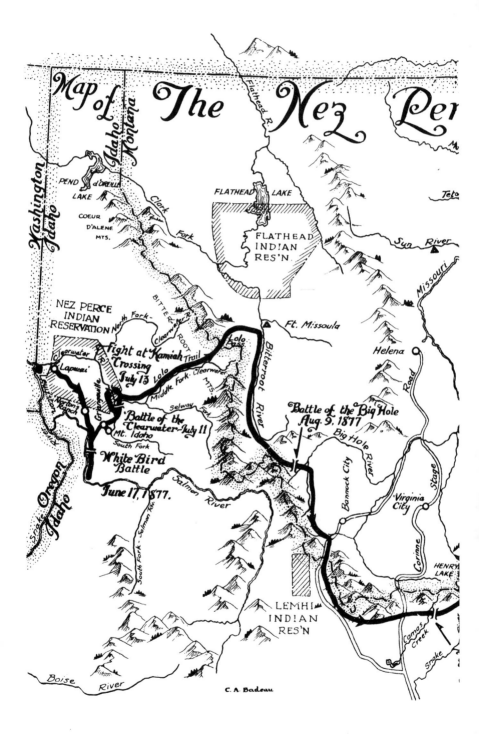

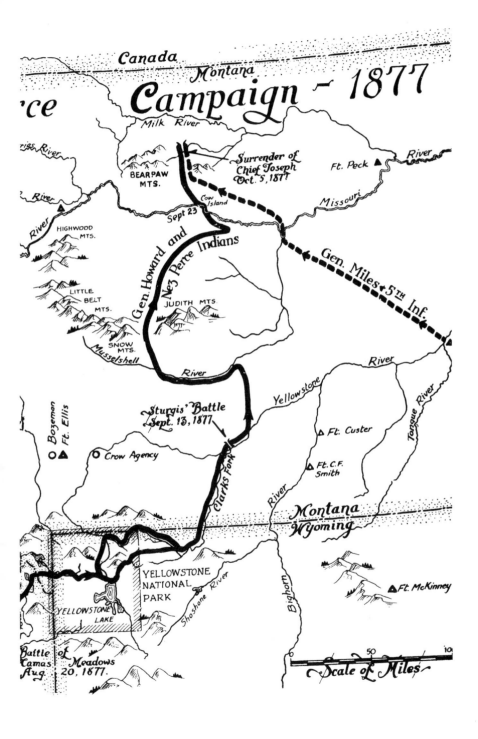

OLLIKUT:

WAR CHIEF OF THE NEZ PERCE

❧ ❧

By
J'Wayne "Mac" McArthur

Many happy trails

J' Wayne McArthur

Copyright 2010, J'Wayne "Mac" McArthur

Printed by Watkins Printing
Logan, Utah

For information, write"
J'Wayne "Mac" McArthur
2737 S Buckboard DR
Franklin, ID 83237

All rights reserved. No portion of the book may be reproduced or
transmitted in any form or by any means, whether electronic or mechanical,
by photocopying, tape recording, or otherwise not stored in a retreival system
without permission of the author.

Author: J'Wayne "Mac" McArthur

ISBN: 978-1-60921-008-3

TABLE OF CONTENTS

ACKNOWLEDGEMENTS

The use of the map is a courtesy given me by Caxton Press. It is a great addition to the book.

I would like to thank all the people that read and commented on the Ollikut manuscript. Ted Rienwald from Pinedale, Wyoming, critiqued the manuscript deleting some of my commas. I have been told I use too many commas. Just being an old cowboy, I write like I hear it in my mind.

The positive feedback given to me by Dr. Lyle G. "Doc" McNeal was such an influence for me to get it finished and in print. He is well steeped in the life and lore of the Nez Perce of that time. He works with the Navajo people to improve their lot.

I traded Norma Bensen Allen a handmade wood burl table for a painting. This painting has been reduced to make the cover for this book. The horse was my horse named Leo and the boy is my son Shawn. Shawn showed in Appaloosa Costume Classes as well as youth classes. Norma's daughter Holly was one of my teaching assistants for the western riding classes I taught at Utah State University while she was studying there. She also posed for many of the pictures in my horse training book. Holly's daughter, Raquel Tarbet, did some of the preliminary art work with two horse pictures.

I would like to thank Jenni Hatch for all the typing she has done. It hasn't been easy keeping up with my writes and rewrites, besides trying to decipher my hand writing while taking care of a husband and two young sons.

The Johnson sisters, Ja Nae and Jessica have produced the pencil drawings for this book. They have worked diligently to get the pictures ready for the book printing. I appreciate their fine work.

INTRODUCTION

I started to get interested in the plight of the Nez Perce Indians back in the 1950's. I chose to write a high school English project on Lewis and Clark. I researched the Lewis and Clark treck and found a lot of Indians helped them in their journey. The ones that interested me the most were the Nez Perce.

In a college English class, I chose to research and write a paper on the Lewis and Clark journey once again. I found myself even more interested in the peaceful Nez Perce Indians.

After my Masters Degree and a six year stint with the Economic Research Service USDA I was hired as an assistant professor in Agricultural Economy at Utah State University. Between research projects, I made time to research the Nez Perce Indians through their peaceful years and through the retreat from five armies over nine battles.

I wrote over two hundred pages on this saga. I had a few people read it. I knew I needed a few more reads so I asked Ken Brewer, a professor in the English Department and Billie Emert, wife of then Utah State University President George Emert. They both gave me good critiques and I reworked the manuscript dropping one chapter and adding two more. I thought I had finished the manuscript in 1976. I had a few nice letters of approval on it. Then I got busy writing research and popular work and just let it sit for the next thirty years.

When I retired in 1997, I started looking at my Ollikut manuscript again. The first person that came to mind for an opinion of my last draft was Billie. I had lost contact until the end of 2009 when a friend located her in Bellingham, Washington. I sent her and her husband, George, a copy of "The Horse Called Spokane: Montana's 1889 Kentucky Derby Winner." They reported they liked that book and Billie suggested she would like another look at Ollikut before it went to print. She put a lot of time and expertise into cleaning up my punctuation. I know it's a better read because of her work.

FOREWORD

I was recently requested by a former outstanding Utah State University faculty colleague, Mr. J'Wayne McArthur, noted writer and cowboy poet to review his book draft entitled "Ollikut: War Chief of the Nez Perce". I have told "Mac" that I sincerely enjoyed this volume about the Nez Perce and that I've read it twice.

Having lived and worked on many Native American Reservations during my life I, like "Mac", have personally witnessed and know of the deep rooted cultural clashes between the dominant culture over the history of the United States and Canada. "Ollikut ..." is a historical fiction book that leans heavily on the side of non-fiction, especially with the core story about the Nez Perce Indians' long journey from their Native Lands in the Pacific Northwest to the Bear Paw's in Montana, while being harassed by the U.S. Army and primarily General Howard.

Personally having grown up in Montana and during my life travels over almost every mile of the pursuit of Chief Joseph and his people their dash for freedom to Canada, I could feel in my spirit and soul the issues, conflicts and intra-tribal friction throughout the entire story. I have also witnessed in modern times inter-tribal friction, but personally prefer the manner with which they resolved these problems within the tribe without the government's intervention which is brought out in "Ollikut: War Chief of the Nez Perce."

Mr. McArthur's book is one that most American's should have the opportunity to read and understand. It presents just one of the many incidents that was inflicted on the resident Native American cultures as the dominant culture moved West in order to satisfy their needs for Mother Earth and her valuable resources.

I really never realized that Chief Joseph and his brother, Ollikut, were so different spiritually and mentally. Ollikut was the war chief and Joseph was the peacemaker. I did additional research on the non-fictional history and found the situation that Mr. McArthur tells in his book to have been true too. The same intra-family conflicts are also seen in today's contemporary American and global cultures as well.

The book is very appealing to all ages from high school students to senior citizens. In the future I would like to see Mr. McArthur author a book on the development of the Appaloosa horse. He does however capture this breed in the closing poem, "The Breed That Wouldn't Die."

As an avocational Western Historian and curator of a large personal Old West Museum, I strongly encourage the reader to read this book while keeping in mind that the fictional components are minimal and the truth of the story lies close to non-fiction in the end.

Dr. Lyle G. "Doc" McNeal, Carnegie Professor
Founder, The Navajo Sheep Project and Livestock Specialist
Animal, Dairy and Veterinary Science Department
Utah State University Logan, Utah

PROLOGUE

This is the story of a small band of Indians who lived in the Wallowa Valley in the corner of Washington, Idaho, and Oregon. They were a very peaceful band of the Nez Perce Tribe. All they wanted in life, was to be free to hunt and fish in the open country. They were forced to flee from their homeland and fight nine battles with five different Army segments. There was no justification for the plight these Indians were forced to endure. Some of the Nez Perce lived through the battles to be imprisoned on a reservation in Oklahoma. Years later, they were returned to the Lapwai reservation to become farmers. This is a historical fiction novel. The people, places and times are true. The activities of some of the people are fiction.

Chapter 1
MISSION SCHOOLING

The Chief of the Wal-larn-wat-kin band of the Nez Perce Tribe, Chief Joseph, had seven children from three different wives. Warriors who had done many great deeds and had much wealth of horses and goods usually had more than one wife. In this way, the greater warriors would reproduce more great warriors. Those men of the tribe who had no great deeds or those without courage had one wife and few sons, or no wives at all.

The chief's youngest wife was named Arenoth. Her first son was called Hin-mah-Too-yah-lat-kekt which meant "Thunder Traveling to Lofty Mountain Heights." He was a good son that helped his mother and played with the younger boys. He was a peace maker and one that everyone enjoyed having in their tepees.

She had another son some seasons later. He was called Ollikut. This son was not interested in helping his mother or sitting in the elders' tepees listening to stories of the past deeds of bragging old men. He was more interested in hunting with the young men. He was a good shot and practiced often to increase his skills.

The Chief's two sons looked so much alike as they matured that often they were mistaken for one another. Old Joseph could easily tell them apart because Ollikut parted his hair on the left side while Joseph parted his on the right side. Ollikut shot his bow holding the bow in his right hand while pulling the string and arrow with his left hand. He shot his rifle with the butt on his left shoulder. This was opposite of Joseph. Indians usually mounted their horses from the right side so they could use their strongest arm holding the mane to swing on with. Ollikut mounted from the left side because his left arm was the strongest. The soldiers also mounted their horses from the left side since they wore their swords on their left side. It made more sense to mount from the left so the sword did not get in the way.

Ollikut was often praised for something his brother had done. Sometimes his brother was blamed for something Ollikut had done, but seldom the reverse occurred. Ollikut was the one that lived from one adventure to another.

The Medicine Man or Dreamer told a story about these two sons that looked very similar:

In the world before, the spirits of many people dwelt. These spirit people had to find a living woman to bear them. The spirits came to this land riding jackrabbits. They would travel around until they found a woman bending over and filling jars with water at the creek. This was a hard trial for the spirit people. It was even harder when they were twin spirits like Ollikut and his brother.

The Dreamer told that when Ollikut and his brother came to this world they were counseled to both get inside the same woman, but when they were hunting for a woman, Ollikut's brother was riding a fast rabbit and he reached the woman first. He got inside quickly and Ollikut couldn't get to the woman before she got up. Because these two spirits were twins in the previous world, they had to have the same mother. That meant Ollikut had to wait a few seasons before he found this same woman bending over filling jars.

Ollikut knew he and his brother looked very much alike, but that was as far as their likeness went. Their father had sent them to the mission school to learn the white man's ways. Their father had been the first Nez Perce to be baptized and given a new name in 1836. He was given the name of Joseph and was known by this name thereafter. His oldest son was baptized and given the same name because he was the eldest son from his last marriage. He was called Young Joseph.

Ollikut had no interest in the missionary teachings. He was interested in learning the ways of the hunters and warriors. He was satisfied listening to the Dreamer who was preaching against the missionaries.

Mr. Spaulding baptized Ollikut and gave him the new name of David. Mr Spaulding told Ollikut how David, in the Bible, had killed his people's enemy, a giant of a man with a sling shot.

Ollikut did not like having a new name, but he did like the idea of David being a warrior. Still, he wouldn't answer to the name David. Even after three winters at the mission, he still told everyone his name was Ollikut. He told them if they wanted him to answer to their calls, then they should call him Ollikut.

Ollikut's mother made up his name. It wasn't a Nez Perce word. She just liked the fresh sweet sounds she put together. At the Spaulding mission, Mrs. Spaulding pronounced his name Ollo-kot. Ollikut did not like her or the sounds she made when using his name. He liked the sounds his mother made when saying his name.

Through the Spaulding records his name was spelled O-l-l-o-k-o-t and that carried down through history.

Spring was coming and soon their father would come to take them home. Joseph would have stayed longer if his father would have let him, but Ollikut was anxious to be in the Wallowa Valley where he was born.

Chief Joseph's band was the first to accept the Christian religion, but some bands had totally adopted the white man's way.

They got twenty acres and a team of horses if they would move to Lapwai reservation and live like a white man. Old Chief Joseph wanted his sons to learn the white man's language and ways, even their religion. After many years, Chief Joseph still had the Bible they gave him when he was baptized even though he couldn't read it. Young Joseph also kept his Bible with his special keepsakes.

Ollikut gave his Bible away as soon as he got back to the Wallowa Valley. Every fall, Mr. Spaulding complained because Ollikut did not have his Bible when he came back to school. He would have to give Ollikut a new one each fall.

"Father, you have come to take us from here," Ollikut said as he met his father at the gate to the mission. It was May 15, 1863.

"Yes, son, I have missed having you to hunt with me. I am not as good a shot as I once was. You seldom miss and that always means the hunt won't be too long," Joseph said.

"I have been waiting for weeks for you to come, but I don't know if Joseph wants to go home."

Mr. Spaulding met Chief Joseph and Ollikut at the school door.

"You have come to take your son home, I see," he said.

"I have come to take both of my sons home."

"I'm not sure Young Joseph wants to go back to your world. He likes living like a white man now."

"That means he has been here too long, I believe," said Joseph.

"Young Joseph accepts this life. He likes talking about religion, government and the white man's way of life. He is a model student and is thought well of by all who know him. I would be happy to send him back to our college. Ollikut is not thought of as well as his brother. He is always playing tricks on other students. He even caused Mrs. Spaulding to be scared. He went out to the outhouse and waited for Mrs. Spaulding to come. She went in the outhouse and sat down. Ollikut started growling like a cougar. He scratched on the back of the outhouse until Mrs. Spaulding came running out. She was screaming and so afraid. She used a bucket for days afterward because she was too scared to go back to the outhouse."

"Why, that was great joke," Old Joseph said.

"It may be in Wallowa, but it isn't in Lapwai. I had to whip him for his action. He is always doing things like that," Mr.

Spaulding remarked.

"Maybe I had better keep Ollikut at home. He is well liked there and he won't get whipped for having fun."

"Mrs. Spaulding is a good teacher. She expects results. She had to reprimand Ollikut for his lack of interest. He is always looking out the window."

"What are you thinking about when you are looking out the window?" Mr. Spaulding asked Ollikut.

"My home at Wallowa and my father," Ollikut said.

"I can understand you thinking about your father, but I can't understand what you see in that valley."

Ollikut thought for a moment then answered, "The Wallowa country is a good country. The Great Spirit put it exactly in the right place. While you are in it, you fare well. When you are out of it, whichever way you travel, you fare worse."

If his father had not come for him, Ollikut had been ready to run away and head for home. His father brought two extra horses for the boys to ride.

"I'll get my bedroll and Joseph and then we will be ready to go," Ollikut told his father.

While they were waiting, Mr. Spaulding once again offered to send Young Joseph to college in the east.

"I know you highly esteem the kind of learning taught in those colleges. The maintenance of my son while there would be expensive. I am sure, therefore, that you mean to do good by your offer and I thank you heartily. But you, who are so wise, must know that different nations have different conceptions of things. I hope you will not take offense if my ideas of the right kind of education do not agree with yours," Joseph said. "Several of our young men have been taught in the colleges of the east where they

14

were instructed in all your knowledge. When they came back to us, however, they were bad runners, ignorant of how to live in the woods, and unable to bear either cold or hunger. They knew not how to build a lodge, take a deer, or kill an enemy. They spoke our language poorly and were not fit to be hunters, warriors nor counselors. They were good for nothing. I am, nevertheless, obliged for your kind offer, though I cannot accept it."

That upset Mr. Spaulding, and he started to once again relate the advantages of the white man's ways but could see the Chief had shut his mind, a common characteristic of the red man.

"I have lived to see civilization brought to my morally clean people and with it profanity, drunkenness, smallpox and wasting venereal diseases. Is it any wonder that I deem the cost far beyond any possible gain from the white man's ways? I know that my people must learn your ways, but that doesn't mean we have to live your way," Joseph told Mr. Spaulding.

Ollikut soon appeared with Young Joseph. Ollikut had changed into his buckskins. He had braided his hair as best he could because it was so short. He had been letting it grow out ever since they cut it shorter when he came to the mission last fall.

Young Joseph was still dressed in his white man's clothes. Ollikut had left his in the dormitory. Joseph's hair was hanging straight to his shoulders. It was bunched up over his forehead as many of the Nez Perce did. At the school, they were not permitted to wear braids. Joseph and Ollikut were fine looking young men. They, like their people, were very handsome. Many of the women were even found beautiful by the white man.

"See, this is what I mean, Joseph keeps his white man's clothes and looks, while Ollikut is back to his Indian ways," Spaulding pointed out.

"I'm sure he will go back to his own people's ways once he gets home," Chief Joseph said.

They mounted their horses and rode off.

Since the mission had been established, many of the Nez Perce came to Lapwai and had taken up farming. They were growing potatoes and other vegetables as well as wheat and feed grains for the animals on the twenty acres they were given. One Indian family had even started an orchard. The Spauldings had set up a crude grist mill to grind the wheat into flour for bread and other cereal foods.

Ollikut did not like living at the school anymore than he liked eating the white man's food. He was accustomed to fresh meat and the camas root for a vegetable. Berries were his dessert.

As the threesome traveled toward home, Ollikut thought of how much he loved the valley of the winding waters known as Wallowa Country. The hills and plateaus were ablaze with color. The blue flowered camas were so numerous that they resembled little lakes from a distance. The cool, pink color of the bitterroot dotted the hills.

The soft breeze off the Pacific felt warm and soothing after the long winter. Snow banks in the pine-dotted hills were melting rapidly. Every creek and rill seemed determined to escape its banks. As the water tumbled down the hills, it brought with it the dark color of the rich soil and stained the swollen Wallowa River.

"Has Sego Lily had her baby yet, father?" Ollikut asked.

"Yes, just a few days ago. You will be surprised to see what a beautiful colt she has produced."

Sego Lily was not an ordinary spotted mare. She was the chosen of all Chief Joseph's mares even though her color was not especially bright. From a colt with a dark body and little white specks over the loin, she had changed colors to white with dark specks over her entire body. It was her speed and endurance as a filly that had brought her favor in the Chief's eyes. Since growing older she had been allowed to roam with the brood band and raise colts. It was a good life for the Chief's favorite mare. The feed was plentiful all year since the winters were mild along the river bottoms. The summers were heavenly on the plateaus, two to three thousand feet above the valley floor, yet within a couple of mile's walk.

Each year Chief Joseph would mate Sego Lily to the finest spotted stallion he had, and each year she produced a spotted colt of high quality. Each mating brought great praise from the Chief. This year, however, Chief Joseph had promised her colt to Ollikut.

Ollikut was big for his age of fifteen summers. He was almost the size of Joseph who was four summers older. They both had smooth, well formed features. They had high cheek bones with a smooth nose, not hawkish like some Indians.

Ollikut's eyes sparkled with life and excitement. Joseph was more thoughtful. He had a worried mark on his forehead already. Joseph was satisfied with a quiet life. He enjoyed fishing more than hunting. Ollikut went hunting every chance he got. He was already the leader of the older boys in camp.

Chief Joseph knew he was proud of both his sons. Joseph had a mild way about him. He was always in control and seldom angered. He was, in turn, to be the Chief someday. He would be the civil leader of the band. Old Joseph knew that Young Joseph would be a good counselor.

Yet a band such as this needed a warrior chief, too. Ollikut was respected as a young warrior and in time he would take his place as a war chief, if war ever came. For now, he was satisfied hunting and working with the young horses.

Until now, Ollikut had hand-me-down horses, but at fifteen it was time for him to start building a herd of his own. Some members of Joseph's band had over 300 horses. His father had told him of one Chief of years past who had personally owned 1500 horses. This was a sign of wealth. Ollikut wanted someday to have a fine herd of spotted horses which meant wealth. Any man with 300 horses was very rich. By selling only the poorer quality of the increase and the old mares from such a herd, a man could continue to have guns and ammunition, as well as any other white man's goods he wanted, and still maintain his 300 head. This was in the back of Ollikut's mind as he looked forward to seeing his colt.

Last spring, because he was to get the next colt, Joseph told Ollikut it was only right that he should choose the stallion to which Sego Lily was to be bred. Ollikut had looked over all the stallions in the Wallowa Valley. They were all fine animals. Had they not been so, they would have been gelded and sold, or used for pack animals. The Nez Perce herds were carefully built by selective breeding. The mediocre animals, scrubs, culls, and worn-out pack animals were kept only for trading to other Indians or to the whites. Next to these in value were the ones used as packhorses and as mounts for women, children and old people. They were usually gentle, well-broke animals of average ability. These groups made up the majority of any horse herd.

The better horses, much fewer in number, were reserved for the men. Many of these were sound, easy-gaited geldings used for ordinary traveling. Such horses did not need to be showy or especially speedy. Rated above them in value were the aristocrats of the herds, the buffalo hunting horses and the war horses.

The previous year, Ollikut searched for a mate for Sego Lily, but none of the stallions satisfied him. He knew one that might. While at the mission school the winter before, he had heard talk of a black stallion named Le Bleu that resided at Spokane House. This stallion had outrun every horse that had raced against him. Horses had been brought from up and down the Columbia River Basin to race him. By outrunning Le Bleu, they could win $200 which was put up by his white merchant owner. If they lost, they had to pay $100.

Ollikut thought that mating a horse with such speed to Sego Lily would surely create an offspring of superior ability. The next task was to find a way to breed Sego Lily to this great running stallion.

The spring before, his father had sent a message to Le Bleu's owner to arrange for this mating. He sent word he would give two of his finest buffalo robes in exchange. The merchant returned a message saying he would have no part in further upgrading Chief Joseph's horse band. They were already some of the strongest and fastest horses in the West.

Ollikut, however, was not one to take "no" for an answer. He had a feeling from the Great Spirit that this mating would produce a "Spirit" horse that would carry him to great deeds. He decided to arrange the mating himself. He asked Running Elk, who had recently been to Spokane House, about the handling of Le Bleu and found that a white lad took the big black stallion out each day for exercise. Ollikut waited until Sego Lily was ready to breed. He then loaded two buffalo hides on her, jumped on his horse and headed for Spokane House.

As Ollikut rode, he thought about what horses meant to his

people. Remembering stories of the days before the Nez Perce had horses, Ollikut wondered what it had been like to be dependent upon fishing in the Clearwater, Snake, and Salmon Rivers for survival.

Once they obtained Spanish horses in 1770 by trading with other Indians from the south, their whole way of life changed. He recalled his father telling him how some of the people had combined their hides and other trade goods and gone to trade for horses, one of which was a white mare with speckles around her nose and eyes. She was in foal which excited the people of the tribe. Members of the tribe would watch her as she grazed, waiting for the birth. This was the mother of the spotted Nez Perce horses, the Spirit horses.

Some of the older Nez Perce, however, had not liked the intrusion of the horse. They wanted no changes in their way of life and remained true to their past. But the younger braves were pleased by the idea of riding instead of walking. They enjoyed the excitement of speed and danger. The hunts were thrilling beyond belief. For these young men, fishing would never do.

As time passed, more and more of the younger members of the tribe took to riding and going east to Sioux country to hunt buffalo. The elders continued to walk. The older people did use the horse as a pack animal, however, in place of the dogs that had been used for so long before. As the new riders grew older and had families, they taught their children to ride, hunt, live off the land, and grow strong on adventure. As they rode east to the plains they encountered the Sioux, a nomadic plains Indian. The Nez Perce adopted many of their ways of life and even some of their customs.

Some bands of Nez Perce, however, never did use horses as

a way of life. They stayed close to their fishing waters and dug camas roots to store for the winter. When the missionaries came, these sedentary Indians were prime prospects for conversion to the Christian religion.

The missionaries taught that the fast horses were evil and would draw their owners into racing, gambling and fighting, which were sins of the highest order. By depriving the Nez Perce of fast horses, the missionaries could keep some of them in one place and change their cultural practices to conform to the white man's ideas of right and wrong.

To be a good Christian, a Nez Perce had to dress and live like a white man. Braids in the men's hair and buckskins were wrong. The missionaries said these were signs of a heathen, not a Christian. The missionaries wanted all trips to the buffalo ground in Montana to be stopped. They recommended to the Indian agent that any family going to the buffalo grounds would have their twenty acres and cabin taken away. While on these trips, the Indians tended to revert to the old ways and then the missionaries had to educate them all over to the white man's ways.

As he rode along leading Sego Lily, Ollikut recalled being told about how his father had such a great desire for stronger medicine that he was the first Nez Perce to be accepted as a convert at the mission at Lapwai (which means "The place where the butterfly dwell"). The mission was run by a Protestant minister named, Mr. Spaulding.

Even though Joseph was baptized a Christian, he had become quite disillusioned with Christianity the past few years. Both Catholics and Protestants were busily trying to obtain converts and were causing much unrest in the tribe. Mr. Spaulding would not permit a Catholic school at Lapwai, thus the Catholics were bitter about the government supported Protestant program.

Chief Joseph was so concerned that when he had taken Ollikut and Young Joseph back to the mission last fall, he cautioned them about religion saying: "Sons, they will teach you to quarrel about God, as Catholics and Protestants do at Lapwai and other places. We do not want to do that. We may quarrel with men about things on earth, but we never quarrel about the Great Spirit. I do not want you to learn that."

That advice stayed with Ollikut. He believed in the Great Spirit his ancestors followed. He did not need more than one God. As he emerged from the timber, he could see Spokane House still at a distance. Giving his horse a nudge in the side, he hurried toward it. He was filled with excitement at having a chance to see the famous Le Bleu.

Arriving late in the afternoon, Ollikut realized he would have to stay the night because Le Bleu would not be taken out until morning. However, he saw the stallion that evening, as he was being led out to water. Seeing Le Bleu in the flesh exceeded Ollikut's expectation. He was a mystic sight. He was taller than most Indian ponies. His color was true black. In the late afternoon sun, he appeared blue as the deep blue waters of the high country lakes. This was indeed the stallion for Sego Lily. Ollikut was taken in with the stallion's strong back and long round hip. He had straight, well-refined legs. His eyes were set wide apart, showing a lot of intelligence.

Ollikut could hardly wait for morning. He made camp in a grove of pines in the direction Le Bleu would be ridden for his morning exercise. Sleep came slowly, Ollikut's mind was filled with visions of the colt Sego Lily would give him and the great horse herd that he could build with this colt as the heart of his breeding. He was sure the foal would be a male colt.

The next morning he hurriedly ate dried meat and prepared camas roots he had brought with him. It did not taste as good as a cooked meal at home, but he had learned on the hunts that the important thing about food was not taste, but whether it gave you strength to pass the tests of the day.

After waiting two hours, he saw the shimmering black stallion galloping toward him. Leaving Sego Lily tied to a tree, he mounted his horse and rode out to intercept Le Bleu. A white lad, about his own age was riding Le Bleu. Ollikut motioned for the boy to pull up but he did not respond. Ollikut rode straight for the black stallion and grabbed a rein. Having lived among the whites at the mission school, Ollikut was able to tell the boy, using the English language, what he wanted.

"I must breed my mare to your stallion. The Great Spirit has told me the offspring of this mating will be mystic. He will carry me into great adventures."

"I'm not supposed to stop and talk to anyone while I'm exercising Le Bleu. They told me to stay away from any other horses while out here."

"You won't have to tell them you even saw me this morning. I will give you two prime buffalo hides if you will let me breed my mare. They are worth much money."

"But how would I explain bringing back the two hides when I get back?"

"You can hide them near here and come back later to pick them up."

"I will let you breed her just once. I won't come this way tomorrow, so you are taking a chance on her settling with just one breeding."

"She has always settled at the end of her heat so I am hoping that will do."

"Hurry and do it, so I won't be late."

That was how Sego Lily had been bred the past spring. This spring Chief Joseph had been checking her often the last week. He could see her belly poking out till it looked like she would burst. Joseph could see she was about ready to foal. Her bag had formed and waxed over a week before, and this morning there was milk dripping from her teats.

As her bag started to get tight with milk, she left the band of mares. This was a time for her to be alone. Many days ago, she had located a nice grassy draw that would make a fine foaling ground. With a spring at the lower end of the draw, she didn't have far to travel for food and water the last few days of waiting.

It had been drizzling rain for the past two days as it does in the Wallowa country in the spring, but this morning was clear and warm. It was a nice day for giving birth. The unborn foal had been quiet through the night, but since Sego Lily had her pre-dawn drink of cold clear water the unborn foal had been kicking and moving. After she walked up the draw to her bed-ground, she laid down for a short rest before grazing some more. Laying down, however, had become a chore.

Before the sun was a quarter of the way up in the sky, she gave birth to a slick, wet, kicking bundle. She began licking her baby, but before she could get much cleaning done he was up on two front legs, back down again, then up on all fours. His legs were wobbly. He bumped up against his mother and found support. All he cared about right then was finding something to eat. Sensing his need, his mother nuzzled him gently toward her hind legs where he could get a whiff of the sweet smell of the sticky colostrum milk dripping from her bag. It didn't take long for him to get hold of a teat and begin sucking.

Chief Joseph approached quietly, so he would not startle Sego Lily. He could see her cleaning the colt as it leaned against her and nursed. It seemed to Joseph that the colt was never going to take enough milk to ease the pressure on her bag. When the colt had satisfied his hunger, he decided to try his legs again. The bed-ground was flat and he did quite well for only being one hour old. Then, he started up the sloping side of the draw and down he went. One side of him just wouldn't work right. It seemed like his legs were too short on one side, or too long on the other. Once he faced downhill it was better, except for his lack of speed control. The next thing he knew he was down in a heap again, but it was getting easier to get up now. After a few minutes of trying his legs, he was back for another snack and then a nap. Joseph was pleased with Sego Lily's baby. It's color was almost mystic. Few horses had color like his.

When he awoke, he was dry and his hair was fluffing up. He was dark brown from his nose to his withers, but from the withers back he was spectacular. His back was white from his withers clean down over his rump. Many large and small black spots were scattered through the white. His tail and mane were black as night and as fuzzy as dandelion seeds in the wind.

Joseph could see he was big, strong, straight-legged and bright in color. He had one other color characteristic that made him even more exceptional. All four legs were black with white stripes that resembled lightening. Only the spotted horses of the Nez Perce produced these unique lightening stripes, and they didn't do it very often.

Joseph was sure Ollikut would be very pleased with this foal.

Especially because he was a male foal to start his herd. He left Sego Lily and her foal and went back to camp.

On the fifth day, Sego Lily heard the dominant mare of the herd squealing in fright. She went to the edge of the draw. She saw five riders coming down upon the band of seventeen horses. They circled around them and headed them in the direction they had come from.

It was lucky for Ollikut that Sego Lily and her foal were in the draw away from the other horses. If she hadn't of been, she and her foal would have been driven away with the others.

Most Indians and many whites coveted the spotted horses of the Nez Perce. They couldn't trade for them easily. The Nez Perce would only trade or sell the less colored and the poorer quality of their herds.

These Indian robbers happened to ride onto the most desired band of mares in the Nez Perce tribe. They were excited to find such a nice band that far from camp.

Chief Joseph and his sons arrived home that evening to the news that the band of his best mares had been stolen. Within the hour, a group of eight warriors had gathered.

Chief Joseph had a fresh mount and right next to him was Ollikut.

"Do you think you should go with us? You have just had a long ride," Joseph said.

"My great war horse was with that band of mares as well as your most desired mare. I must go in search of the horses, just as you must."

Young Joseph was not interested in any more riding that day for it was beginning to get dark. He was ready for a good night's sleep.

The ten riders were lucky they had a full moon to search in. Two good trackers had started tracking the stolen band as soon as they discovered the mares were missing.

"Father, how much of a head start do you think the thieves have?"

"I was told the tracks looked a day old when they discovered the band missing. They can't travel too rapidly with the mares and colts, but Sego Lily and her foal were in the band. It would be hard for her foal to keep up on a retreat."

This troubled Ollikut. He hadn't even seen his colt and now he might not survive this misadventure. The group climbed up out of the Wallowa Valley to the plateau above. It was light enough that the tracks of the thieves were visible on close inspection.

They had ridden for three hours when they came to a rocky area. The tracks disappeared once the band was on the rocks. They split up in three directions to search for more tracks. Within a few minutes, one of the group hollered out. The rest of the group converged to the spot the yell had come from.

The two trackers had left a piece of white cloth on a bush to mark the direction they should follow. This was a common method Indians used when tracking in divided parties.

The night's ride was beginning to show on Joseph and Ollikut. They needed some rest and so did the other warriors. They picketed their horses and then laid down for a quick nap. They slept for two hours and got up. After eating a little dried meat, they were mounted and following a deer trail among the rocks. It was starting to get light. They were on softer ground and now they could see the tracks again.

Ollikut could see a set of horse tracks that were a little different. The left front hoof print turned in and both back hoof prints toed out. This must have been made by a rider bringing up the rear.

"Did you see that top hoof print made by a horse being ridden? He was a poor traveler."

You are very observant my son. That horse will tire first. The mares will also tire from being pushed so hard. They will have to slow down and maybe stop to let them rest. This will give us a chance to catch up to them."

By mid-day, they came up on a meadow where the thieves had spent the night. It appeared the thieves weren't in much of a hurry now. They had made a fire.

Ollikut knew they had covered a lot of country in a short time. He was still watching for the poor traveling horse's hoof prints.

Soon they saw one of the two advanced trackers coming their way.

"The thieves are up on that plateau and are a short distance into a meadow. They are letting the mares rest and eat."

"Where are they camped?" Joseph asked.

"They are up by that small grove of trees. You can't surprise them by coming up on them from this direction."

"Some of us can ride around to the draw on the west. It looks like there is tree cover we can use to get closer. Ollikut, you and two others can surround the horses to control the mare band once we start shooting."

Joseph and his warriors had rifles and would shoot to kill once they were close enough. Most likely, Ollikut thought, the thieves would have guns, too. All he had was his bow and arrows. He didn't think he would get that close to the fighting anyway.

In a short time, Ollikut heard the rifle shots ring out. The mares' and colts' heads sprang up and they started milling around. Ollikut and his two helpers circled around the band to settle them down.

In the corner of his eye, Ollikut saw a rider riding hard to the east. He turned his horse and was in pursuit. As soon as he crossed the thieves trail, he saw the tracks of the poor traveling horse they had been following.

This thief did not have a fast horse. Ollikut was gaining on him. He saw the thief turn and point his rifle. A bullet flew past, making a whistling sound.

Ollikut settled an arrow on his bow string and drew back. He let it go and ducked as he heard another bullet whistle by. The thief screamed with pain as he rolled off his horse.

Ollikut had set another arrow into his bow string as he rode close to the downed Indian. The thief rolled over with the rifle pointed at Ollikut. In an instant Ollikut slipped off the back of his horse, keeping his horse between him and his enemy. He heard the sound of the rifle again. This time he felt a fire in his lower thigh. The thief had shot under his horse's belly. That spooked the horse and it ran off, so now Ollikut was looking into the eyes of the thief. He let go of the arrow and it sung as it sped through the distance between him and his enemy. The arrow buried deep into the thief's chest. He fell forward and was dead when he hit the ground.

Ollikut looked down at his leg and realized he was bleeding. Taking a rag out of his bag, he covered the wound and wrapped it tight.

As Joseph rode up, he realized what had happened.

"Are you hurt, my son?"

"I have been shot, but it is not bad. I have wrapped the wound so I can ride home."

"We killed four more thieves over in the grove. Now they are all dead. They won't steal horses again."

"Did you see Sego Lily? I didn't find her with the band of mares."

"We will look for her and her colt on the way home. The thieves may have left her and the colt somewhere, if they couldn't keep up."

The ride home was long and painful, but Ollikut couldn't stop thinking of what had happened back on the plateau. He wasn't sure that was what he had wanted to happen, but there was nothing else he could have done once he started shooting.

The mares and the thieves' horses were driven closer up the valley towards camp once they got back. Sego Lily saw them coming but did not follow. Ollikut saw her in the draw and rode over to see his colt. What a happy moment when he realized they were safe. He followed the other warriors into camp. Now he was a warrior also and had done a great deed to count in his coup. Plus, he had the horse of the thief he had killed and could use it for trading.

The next day Young Joseph approached Ollikut.

"I understand you killed an Indian yesterday. Is that true?"

"Yes, I killed a horse thief. Once he started shooting at me, I had no other way to act."

"How did it make you feel to kill a man?"

"Better than if he had killed me."

"That man may have had a wife and children. What do you feel for them?"

"She should have married a smarter horse thief and he wouldn't be dead."

"I can see your heart is not heavy. You have been taught at the mission that killing is bad. Don't you believe these teachings?"

"Our people are peaceful and have not been warred upon for many years. Their fathers knew of these battles. They counted it an honor to count coup on their enemy. If there had been another choice, I would not have killed the thief, but I had no choice. The other warriors praise me for this action. You condemn me. I prefer their praise. One day you may also have to kill to protect what is yours. Will you just stand by or will you fight?"

"I hope that day doesn't come. The choice would be hard for me to make. I'm not sure what I would do."

"I sure wasn't going to turn the other cheek. He had already shot me once."

Sego Lily did not return to the band for more than a week. She grazed in the draw watching her new foal grow stronger and more agile by the day. She waited until he could run at full speed, slide and pivot around and be back at full speed again in a few swift jumps. Then he would be ready to be introduced to the band of horses and learn to survive the pushing, biting and kicking that he would have to deal with.

Life in the band was a real adventure for the new colt. The very first thing when he and his mother entered the band was for him to be inspected. All the horses gathered round and sniffed, nudged and snapped at him. All he could do was chomp his gums and whinny for Sego Lily. His mother had gone through this with so many colts already that she was much more relaxed than he was. The other horses were just looking him over and wouldn't hurt him on purpose. But if the horses got too excited and started pushing and kicking at each other, her colt might get stepped on. She finally moved in with her ears back and teeth showing, whipping her tail a little as she came. The rest of the band knew better than to argue with a mare who had a new foal so they drifted off to graze. The mare and foal found a place to themselves to rest.

The six other new foals in this band were a week to a couple of weeks older than he was, but he had no trouble playing and keeping up with them after the first week. He was big for his age and growing stronger every day. Each day the colts would romp and play and race around the meadow. He could outrun the other colts whenever they were racing. He appeared to have an inner drive to take the lead when they ran.

While the colts were playing in the meadow, they came upon a little, black ball with a white stripe. All the colts stopped and responded to their inborn inquisitiveness.

One colt stepped right up and lowered his head to smell. Up came a tail on the black ball. This made the colt jump back. Another colt came forward and was just about to reach down and smell when Sego Lily's colt reached out and bit him on the rump. The colt jumped with fright and lit right over the top of the black ball. At that moment all the colts learned what little, black balls with white stripes do when they are startled.

The skunk's tail went up again and shot a stinky perfume all over the colt that had jumped on him. The smell was enough to choke even a horse. All the colts started to run. A quarter mile would surely get them away from the smell. Instead, everywhere they went they could still smell the skunk. The colt that had lit on the skunk was quite unpopular for about a week after that. Unpopular or not, he still wanted to play, so the rest of the colts just had to bear it until the smell wore off.

From that time on, Sego Lily's colt never bothered little black balls with white stripes. He had learned to be leery of any little moving thing in the meadow. Even a rabbit jumping up from the underbrush would put him to flight. He soon found his best defense against unexpected danger was to run. His sliding stops, fast turns and burst of speed had already saved him more than once from being kicked. The older mares liked to bite and kick to get their way, but they were too lazy to burst out at full speed after the colt. As long as he was alert, he could play just about anywhere he wanted and still get away from cranky horses that didn't enjoy his antics.

The next day some odd creatures that looked like his mother on the bottom but had something tall sticking up above started coming close. These were mounted braves from camp. They were making sounds that the colt had not heard before. Spooked by the sounds, the whole band of horses started moving toward the river. The colt had been to the river to drink with his mother and had become accustomed to its sounds and smells. They drank in the calm eddies, but had not ventured into the fast water.

The braves intended to move them across the river where the grass was taller. It would be dangerous for the colts if they did not stay calm. As they approached the river, the horses stopped and drank. The braves waited a few minutes, then started yelling again. The mares without colts were the first to enter the river. The water was swift and the rocky riverbed was slick and hard on their feet. They crossed where the river was wide and not as deep or swift as in the narrows. The mares had crossed the river many times in their life and were not concerned for themselves, but in order to assist their foals, each mother waited her turn, then pushed her colt in on the up-current side and quickly got in below the colt. The colt then was washed against the mare's shoulder and side where it floated as they crossed the river.

Sego Lily had crossed the river with her other colts, but none of them had been as large and active as this one. As she pushed him into the river, he started kicking and trying to get his footing. Before she could get below him he was being washed downstream. Even though the river was relatively shallow at this crossing, it was too deep for him to reach the bottom. The water was in his eyes and ears, and most dangerous, it was coming in his nose.

With a big kick from his back feet he pushed himself up to the surface. Trying hard to use his feet as he had when walking he found that he was getting closer to the other side. He tried to turn his head to the other shore and up toward the other horses. By moving his feet faster he was able to move through the water more in the direction he wanted. After a few more moments, his feet touched some rocks. Getting his footing, he scrambled for the shore but the bank was too steep. He could not see the other horses. He had been carried about fifty yards farther down the river. He started whinnying with fright.

As Sego Lily reached the other bank, she broke from the band and ran down the riverbank whinnying for her colt. Soon Sego Lily was above him on the bank. She moved downstream about ten yards where the bank was eroded by the entrance of spring run-off waters. Moving down the bank, she entered the water and worked her way toward him. As soon as he saw her, he tried to move toward her, but he lost his footing and under he went. Up he came again shaking his head to clear the water out of his ears. The current quickly carried him to his mother's side where the footing was better. With her behind him, bumping him up the bank, he was able to get onto dry land again. This was just the beginning of his education.

Chapter 2

THE MEETING

Ollikut's wound was not too serious. He only limped when someone was watching. He had become someone everyone wanted to talk to. The young men even honored him as a hero.

All Ollikut wanted to do was ride over to the meadow where the horse band had been moved so he could see his colt. He had been riding out to watch the colt play in the meadow quite often. Ollikut was glad he was home and not at the mission. He liked wearing his buckskins instead of pants and shirts that made all the Indian boys look alike.

He spoke the Nez Perce tongue at camp. He felt like an Indian, not a white man. He was proud of his braids and buckskin clothes.

Young Joseph wore white man's pants and spoke the white man's words with those of the band that spoke that way. He had accepted many of the thoughts of life that the white man preached. Ollikut realized that they were quite different. Yet, he hoped that would never come between their friendship.

As Ollikut rode up to the band of mares, he could see only Sego Lily's colt's full white blanket with big, black spots and lightning on his legs. That was the colt that really caught Ollikut's eye. It wasn't so much his color as his size and balance. Ollikut knew that this was his "Spirit" colt.

None of the colts had come into close contact with man yet, except for the river crossing. They were all very apprehensive of the buckskin clad figure moving toward them. His colt would have no part of this new creature on two feet who kept trying to get closer.

Finally, Ollikut sat down in the meadow about fifty feet away from the band of horses. It was almost as though he had turned to rock. He had not hurt the colts, so Sego Lily's colt's inquisitive nature got the best of him. He circled to the outside of the band, then slowly walked out towards Ollikut's stationary form. He tossed his head up and down hoping his movements would scare the intruder. Instead Ollikut just sat still. The colt came within ten feet of him and paused.

Ollikut studied the structure of his prize possession with great intensity. He wanted to see if the colt equaled the vision he had of it. First, he noticed this was a male foal. That was good for in a few years he could be the sire of many more colts. The broad forehead with well set eyes indicated intelligence.

This colt with the big white rump had a short back and full, round hips that carried down into wide stifles. The long, lean gaskin muscles would fill out with time and work. Oh, what a fine colt, Ollikut thought. No one could ask for more. Yet, the colt did have more. He had straight lean legs with the rarely seen lightning stripes. It was said that the Great Spirit placed these marks on the fastest horses he sent to the Nez Perce. Ollikut believed in signs and was a follower of the old ways. He thought that one day soon this colt might even take him into battle. He was pleased to have such a fine colt to face hardships he sensed were coming to his people.

Ollikut had observed all this in a matter of moments, then moved his head. Instantly the colt swung and rolled to his left in a 180 degree spin, dropping his hips and digging the dirt with his hooves as he made two jumps and was at full speed back toward the small band.

The colt had thrown so much dirt and dust that Ollikut instinctively jumped to get out of the way. Seeing the intruder standing on two legs again, the colt ran over to Sego Lily and bumped up against her for reassurance. Then, ducking his head under her neck, looked again at the intruder.

Ollikut was satisfied with his colt. Next he knew he must find a name for such a marvelous animal. This was not something that could be done without a lot of thought. If the colt was to be his personal mount, he must have a proper name.

As he walked back to camp, Ollikut thought of all the horses he had known or heard of. He said their names out loud. None of them seemed to fit. Returning back to camp, he encountered his father.

"Father, what name would be the best for such a fine colt?"

Chief Joseph thought for a moment and then said, "For what purpose did you mate Sego Lily to Le Bleu?"

Ollikut immediately said, "I wanted a horse for going fast."

"Why not name him Henawit."

"Henawit means 'going fast'. That is a fine name," said Ollikut.

The next day Ollikut returned to the meadow to watch his colt play. He was eager to start the colt's training, but it was not the practice to work with colts until they were weaned in the fall. Then they could be caught, broken to lead, and gentled all at the same time.

To see Henawit run circles around the other colts brought tingles all through Ollikut's body. He had never seen a colt so beautifully built with such high colors. This was truly a mount for a chief or lead warrior. Ollikut wanted just to touch this bundle of muscle and fluff so he slowly moved around in the little band until he was directly behind Sego Lily. She didn't make a move because she didn't worry about his presence. He could see the colt but the colt couldn't see him.

One quick jump and Ollikut had hold of the colt. Another quick jump and the colt had broken his hold and put both hind feet in his belly. Ollikut went down, rolling with pain and out of air. The little band of horses spooked off a few yards then went back to grazing. Henawit had learned that you kick and check later when you are startled. In that way a coyote or bobcat could be repelled before he had a chance to sink his teeth into a leg.

After rolling on the ground for some time and gasping for breath, Ollikut finally sat up and looked around. Not more than ten feet from him stood Henawit. The colt was again inquisitive as to what was rolling around in the grass. He had not seen Ollikut before or after he kicked so he did not connect the rolling object on the ground with the attack from the rear.

Ollikut didn't know what to do. He was still hurting from the sting of those sharp little hooves. Ollikut was tempted to pick up the stick next to him and let the colt have one right back. He knew that would only make Henawit more scared and flighty. Instead of throwing the stick, he pulled some grass and just stood there with the grass in his hand. The colt was quite full of his mother's milk as well as grass that grew in abundance in the meadow, yet the sight of Ollikut pretending to nibble on it made it desirable. By holding the grass out to the colt he could keep his attention. Then he would take it back and pretend to eat it, slowly taking a step toward the colt.

After Ollikut took a few steps, Henawit would back up a step and shake his head up and down to see if he could scare Ollikut.

Everything was calm and quiet. Ollikut had not hurt him. Soon the colt got closer. Ollikut could see the colt's brave spirit coming forth. Sticking his neck way out he pulled a few blades of grass from Ollikut's hand. That was quite easy to get and nothing happened, so the colt just moved in a couple more steps to get it all.

Just at that moment Ollikut grabbed the colt around the neck and away they both went. He had heard the tales of the Indians that got close enough to a wild horse to jump on his neck and stay with him until he quit bucking and running and in this way capture and tame the horse. This time it wasn't working, because about every other jump the colt came down on his moccasin-covered toes with those little sharp hooves.

The colt's neck was small and slippery. Henawit pushed it close to the ground which make it hard to hold. After about seven jumps, the colt was on top and Ollikut was on bottom. Soon Ollikut had had enough. Letting go was no small matter. Since dropping down to the ground would put him right under the colt. When Ollikut finally let go, he rolled to the side. Henawit let go with the back foot closest to Ollikut just as he rolled over. He caught Ollikut right on the rear end with a solid blow.

Ollikut knew when he was whipped. Pulling himself up, he began picking things up. A moccasin here, a knife over there and a headband . . . no where to be seen. He looked for a minute and finally found it in some trampled grass. From that day on he knew he had a colt that would bow to no man unless a real bond of friendship was built. He was a mystic horse with a mind of his own.

As he hobbled back to camp, he thought again how lucky he was to live in the Wallowa and not down on the farms of Lapwai.

He felt heartsick for his school friends who had never lived in the hills or ridden the fast, spotted horse. Their lives were destined to be hard, seeking out an existence from a twenty-acre plot of ground. They would never know the thrill of the hunt or the feeling of new life when a colt was born.

Ollikut's father was a wise man and had been very careful to keep the best horses and cattle. Only selling what they didn't want had brought in enough goods, gold and currency so his small band of Indians were quite well-to-do. Instead of twenty acres per family, Joseph's Nez Perce controlled over seven million acres of grazing and timber land. Their horses numbered in the thousands as did their cattle. The pride and aloofness that his father showed the white man, as well as his oratorical power, frightened many white men to the point of wanting to banish him and his band from the Wallowa. Ollikut knew his father was aware of this jealousy and was determined to maintain the 1855 treaty which he felt would protect all his people.

Chapter 3
TRIALS OF A COLT

Ollikut realized that he must leave Henawit alone for the summer. He could not move all the mares to the breaking pen every time he wanted to catch him. He could also see that Henawit wanted no part of him right now. With all the older colts that had to be broke and the many hunting trips to go on, he would be busy anyway.

All summer Henawit played in the meadow with the other colts. He did have some close calls though. One evening a small pack of young wolves attacked him and three other colts while they were romping in the meadow about a quarter mile away from the mares. The wolves came in so quickly and quietly. They had surrounded the colts before being detected.

The snarling canines were hungry and knew the small colts would be much easier to bring down than a mare. The oldest of the young wolves came in fast, and on the first attack tore into the back leg of one colt. One of the wolves came at Henawit. He fired both hind feet at the wolf sending him sprawling on the ground. Kicking was just not enough because there were too many. Turning to face two young wolves that were between him and the mares, Henawit lowered his head, bared his teeth and charged. The other colts turned to follow. As he reached the wolves one grabbed for his throat, but Henawit reached out with a front foot and caught him on the head. The wolf went down with a thud. The other two hesitated just long enough for Henawit to jump between them, and in two more jumps he was at full speed. The other colts followed.

The colt that had been bitten earlier was slowed down by the pain from the torn muscle. This was all the advantage the wolves needed. They jumped at the colt. One had hold of a hind leg and the other had the colt's throat. The momentum of their attack knocked the colt to the ground. Before he could get up the rest of the wolves were in for the kill.

Henawit and the mares ran down to the creek until the wolves were out of sight. Henawit soon settled down, but the fear did not leave him for sometime. He could sense what had happened. One of his own was no longer with the band.

Another close call came when the band of horses he was with was being driven across the river again. Henawit was bigger but no less afraid of the fast water. As he approached the water he hesitated, but the horse behind him was coming fast and knocked Henawit into the water. If there had been a way to avoid going in the water he would have found it, but he was in now. His legs had grown since the last crossing. That made the river seem less deep. He was able to keep his feet on the slippery, rocky bottom and didn't need to swim. The crossing wasn't as bad this time, but the horses were bunching up at the edge of the water where the bank was a bit of a jump. Henawit wanted to get out of the water as fast as he could so he waded downstream only to find a wet, muddy mire there. He tried to crawl out of the bog, but the more he tried the deeper he sank in the mud. Finally, all he could do was whinny.

A brave finally saw him and tossed a rope over his head. Then the brave started to pull. Every muscle in Henawit's neck was stretched. Then, with a couple of lunges he began to rise from the bog. With all his strength he pushed again . . . out he came. He was covered from nose to tail with the grey-black muck. Every muscle in his body ached from strain and he was exhausted.

There was still one small problem. He had a rope around his neck. The brave was not sure how to get it off either. Knowing this colt was more than one man could handle, he called another driver to help. With one on the end of the rope, the other slowly worked his way towards the colt. Henawit fought to get away but the more he fought the tighter the rope became and the harder it was to get air. After all the strain he had been through, he was still gasping for breath anyway.

The rope got tighter with each jump he made. He started getting dizzy from the lack of air. All of a sudden, the Indian rode up, grabbed the rope around his neck and off came the rope! Gasping for air, he stood spraddle-legged waiting for his eyes to focus clearly. After a couple of minutes had passed, he regained his sense of balance and sight. He returned to his mother. He was happy to be free again.

Chapter 4
THE QUEST

It was time for Ollikut to go to the Mountain to seek his power. His brother Joseph had gone two summers before. He had told Ollikut that he had a hard time surviving the ordeal. He was out of his head for two days from hunger and exhaustion. The Spirits told him in a dream that he would have to guide his people over a long journey with many hardships.

Ollikut wondered what the Spirit would tell him. He rode high up the mountain. After a day and a half he found a meadow with a stream running through it. He hobbled his horse so it could graze and drink while staying close for the return trip.

That afternoon he built a fire with the flint he had learned to strike. At home, they used the white man's matches which were much faster. He had not brought the white man's supplies with him.

The night was cool up high on the mountain. The fire felt good. He knew that tomorrow he would have to travel farther up into the mountain and seek his quest.

As dawn broke, Ollikut was up eating a small amount of dried meat he had brought with him. He knew this would only last him a couple of days, so he must conserve it.

He remembered Joseph telling him how he climbed up some steep rock cliffs and couldn't get down the same way. He had to keep climbing until an eagle showed him the way out of the rock cliffs. He knew the animals had great spirits, too. He wondered if one would help him in his quest.

Ollikut hiked up into the hills farther that day. About dark, he came upon a young wolf pup. It was a yearling and had about half of its growth. It was dragging one of its hind legs. Ollikut could see an arrow sticking through its leg. The head of the arrow had gone all the way through the leg.

The wolf pup was exhausted and looked half starved. Ollikut worked his way as close as he could, then the pup drug himself away a couple of steps. Taking a piece of dried meat, he sat down and pretended to eat it, like he had done with Henawit.

Hunger and exhaustion was overcoming the pup. He dragged himself a few feet closer then collapsed. Ollikut hurriedly broke the arrowhead off of the end and pulled the arrow shaft back out of the wound. He poured some water over the wound and washed it out. Ollikut wasn't sure the pup would live, but he cleaned the wound area up as best as he could. He had used over half of his supply of water. Still, he poured some in the pup's mouth. The pup gurgled a little as it choked the water down.

It felt good to Ollikut to see life coming back into the pup. He saw the pup open his eyes. It was as if he knew that Ollikut had given his life back to him. There was no aggression in the eyes, just calmness. Moving back a couple of steps, Ollikut sat back down to see if the pup would survive. He pulled out the dried meat and took a bite. The pup watched for a moment then crawled one step closer to Ollikut. Reaching out, he offered the pup a bite of the meat. The pup reached out and took the piece of meat Ollikut offered him. He chewed and swallowed it. Looking up, he came eye to eye with Ollikut

The story tellers had told of meetings with wolves and said that if you looked at them eye to eye, they would become aggressive, showing their dominance. Ollikut had always looked eye to eye at the dogs in camp. He wanted them to see his dominance was there, too. He didn't back down to them, and they came to respect and trust him. He also did the same with the horses. When he went to catch a horse, he looked straight into its eyes, rather than letting it think it had the power.

Holding out another piece of meat, he offered the pup another bite. Scooting a step closer, the pup took the meat and swallowed it. The meat was almost gone. It wouldn't last until the next day, let alone the rest of the week.

When Ollikut spread out his blanket on the ground, it startled the pup. The pup got up on all fours and slunk off to a nearby tree. Ollikut laid down on some grass and covered himself with the blanket.

As Ollikut awoke he could feel the cold morning air. Rolling up his blanket, he looked around not expecting to see the pup, but to his surprise the pup was still laying by the tree. He wasn't dead because Ollikut could see his yellow eyes following him.

He knew he must find some food and water to replenish his short supply. As he started walking through the trees, the pup stood up on all four feet and started to follow. After a short walk, Ollikut came to a stream where he filled his water bag. The pup took a big drink then another. Ollikut knew if he hadn't helped the wolf, it wouldn't be alive. That made Ollikut feel real good.

The pup sniffed the air and started to walk into the timber. He didn't go far then turned and took two steps towards Ollikut, then turned and started walking again. Was he just saying goodbye, Ollikut wondered. No, he was doing it again. The pup wanted Ollikut to follow him.

By now, the pup was walking much better. Having the arrow removed took much of the pain away. The pup's nose went up again and he sniffed. He moved out on a slow trot so Ollikut started trotting behind him. There it was, a half eaten deer. The pup stood a ways back as Ollikut sliced off a few lean pieces of meat. He sliced a couple more off and sat them a few steps away for the pup. He didn't want to throw the meat to the pup because he was afraid it would scare him.

After they had both eaten their fill, Ollikut sat down to rest. He could see the pup wanted to get closer but was still afraid. Ollikut talked to the pup in the Nez Perce tongue. It was a soft, melodical tone that soothed the pup. Soon Ollikut slid closer and the pup moved closer.

The coyote was thought of by most Indians as a wily animal. The storytellers told of the coyote stealing any meat that was left out, but it was afraid to be seen. The wolf was revered as a brave heart, but they still feared him. There were many stories of the white man about wolves being killers of anything that moved, except the bear.

The half-wolf pups that lived around camp could be tamed to a point. Yet, they always kept their timid wolf ways. Ollikut had two that were his friends. He didn't abuse them and they didn't abuse him.

This pup was timid but he did want to be friends. Ollikut looked into his eyes and could read the true spirit of this pup. He was a kind spirit that would trust another kind spirit.

Ollikut had to go forward to his quest. The pup followed him up the trail. By mid-day, they were both getting hungry. Ollikut stopped and sat down on a log. He pulled out the sack with the raw meat in it. He took his knife and sliced off the drier pieces for himself and set a couple of the rawer pieces on the end of the log for the pup. It wasn't long before the pup was eating the meat only an arms length away from Ollikut. He figured right there he had a friend.

The deer trail got narrow and had some rock over hangs on it. The pup was moving on ahead. Half way across the rocky hill the pup stopped and sniffed the air. He sniffed again and started growling. Ollikut slipped an arrow into the string on his bow.

They hadn't walked over ten steps when a shriek came from the ledge above the trail. A cougar came flying towards Ollikut, catching him in the chest. There was no chance of using a bow. It was all he could do to get to his knife. They were rolling over and over and the cougar's legs were wrapped around him. He felt teeth bite into his shoulder and claws were digging into his ribs. He could hear the pup howling and feel him grab the cat by the back

of his neck. Ollikut was slashing and jabbing the cougar's stomach and chest all he could, but it wasn't enough. The pup dove for the neck of the cougar and bit down hard as Ollikut buried his knife deeper into the cougar's chest. He could feel the cougar releasing his grasp. All at once he was free, but the cougar had the pup's head in its mouth. He heard the bones crush as the cougar bit down. The cougar didn't move or make another sound. One of the knife thrusts must have hit an artery close to the heart. The cougar was dead, but so was the pup.

Ollikut passed out. It was the next day when Ollikut started to come to his senses. He couldn't use his arm and shoulder because of the bites from the cougar, but the wounds had stopped bleeding. He crawled to a tree and leaned against it . His back was sore from the claw marks. He had to lean away from the tree to quit hurting.

As he sat there he remembered the dream he had while he was in the spirit world. He was told that he was to be a leader of the warriors and fight many battles to save his people. The spirit told him even though he was great in battle and would kill many white men, he would not be remembered after his death.

Ollikut finally got to his horse and with the help of a big rock, got mounted. He had buried the wolf pup with rocks as best as he could. He cut off one of the paws of the cougar as proof of his quest.

Once he was home, he told of his ordeal and showed them the paw and the cuts on his shoulder and back, but he didn't tell of his spirit dream. It didn't sound real. The Nez Perce were at peace with the whites. There was no war and none was expected.

He did remember the wolf that gave its life to save his. The wolf pup had been a true friend.

Chapter 5

UNREST IN THE WALLOWA

With the discovery of gold in 1861 along Orofino Creek, a tributary to the Clearwater River, came ten thousand prospectors. The eastern part of the Wallowa was crowded with more whites than the total population of the Nez Perce nation. The miners had completely disregarded every article of the 1855 treaty in their pursuit of the treasure.

The Nez Perce demanded that the whites be removed in accordance with the 1855 treaty. The whites in return were also pushing for the Nez Perce to be moved to a smaller, less valuable reservation.

It was almost impossible for the government to get that many miners off the land when the smell of gold was in their nostrils. With this in mind, the superintendent of Indian Affairs for Washington territory, Calvin H. Hale, called a treaty council with all the Nez Perce on May 15, 1863. This council was to be held at the military post of Fort Lapwai which had been built the previous autumn.

The drain on government funds for fighting the Civil War depleted the U.S. coffers so badly that the $200,000 in goods promised to the Nez Perce in the 1855 treaty never got to them. About $60,000 had actually been allocated for the entire tribe. Joseph had told his people in the Wallowa to accept nothing from the Indian agent so they would owe no debt to the white man.

Upon learning of the upcoming council, Chief Joseph told his two sons they could accompany him to Lapwai when the time came. This pleased them. They enjoyed going to Lapwai to see their friends from missionary school and visit the trading post. They each took some trade goods so they could barter for the things they wanted.

Upon arriving at Lapwai, Chief Joseph went right to the council. He had intentionally timed his trip so he would arrive one day after the council was to begin. He never wanted it said that the white man told Joseph when to come and when to go.

The second day at the council, Chief Joseph was speaking in the meeting. Ollikut and Young Joseph were discussing the problems that existed between the whites and the Nez Perce. They both knew how much the 1855 treaty meant to their father. The honoring of this treaty was the last hope he had of retaining control of the Wallowa country.

"Why can't we have our own land?" asked Ollikut.

Joseph thought for a moment then said, "Many white men would like to use the Wallowa to farm, raise cattle, and mine as they are now starting to do. As long as we are there, they can't do these things freely. Father helped put together and signed a treaty in 1855 that was good. It gave us the Wallowa with all the timber, furs and grass. No white settlers were to live within its boundaries. Now they say they need more land and ask us to sell our land to them."

"How much land do they want?" asked Ollikut.

"Father said they wanted seven out of every eight pieces of land we have. They want the best lands for pasturing horses and the places where the miners are," said Joseph.

"They want to leave us only what they do not desire," replied Ollikut.

"The government said we have too much land for so few

people while the whites need more land because of their increasing number," said Joseph.

Ollikut broke in, "But father said he would sell no land. That's why he took none of their goods. We must keep the land for our people yet to come."

"This is true, Ollikut," said Joseph, "but sometimes we must bend so we do not break."

"But Joseph, after you bend so many times there is no need to break because you can't stand up anymore," replied Ollikut. "I know we both agree with father. He wants peace and the Wallowa. It is just not clear in my mind, Joseph, what will you be willing to sacrifice if we can't have both?"

Joseph thought for quite a few moments, then replied, "Let us hope that such a choice is not needed."

In his mind Ollikut knew the choice he would make. He would fight before he let the white man have his grandfather's land. He did not trust them. He had seen the treaties broken and heard the white man's lies. In his heart he felt that this treaty would end no better than the ones before, but he still hoped.

While their father was at the council, Ollikut and Joseph visited with many old friends. Joseph spent most of the time with Aye-at-wai-at-naime, Good Woman. Good Woman was the daughter of Chief Whisk-tasket of the Nez Perce in Lapwai. Ollikut was not looking for a wife, so he renewed friendships with many young men and women at Lapwai.

The treaty council was not going well. The whites wanted to pay $.08 an acre and buy all but 784,996 acres of the 6,932,210 the Nez Perce now controlled. Chief Joseph wanted the Wallowa protected from white invasion. He knew the Wallowa was the best livestock raising area for hundreds of miles. Unfortunately the white men knew this, too. Also, there was the gold in the hills and the trapping was prime. If the white man came in, he would plow the pastures and meadows, trap out all the fur animals, and the game would disappear. This would leave the Indians practically nothing to live on. This could not be.

As the council wore on, Mr. Spaulding kept insisting that the fast horses should be taken away from those owning them. He informed the council how that spring General Wright was able to control the Indians on the lower Snake River by killing all their horses.

"He shot over 700 horses. The Indians had not a horse to hunt on. He killed them all. That's what we need to do to the Nez Perce horses. Maybe then they wouldn't think they are better than us. Then they would be forced to earn a living on the twenty acres farms or to work for a laborer's wage at the mill. In this way they would learn to live like a white man," he said.

This was his supreme goal.

Becoming quite concerned about being forced to live like the white man and having his horses taken away, Chief Joseph arose and spoke:

"The Great Spirit made the white man and the Indian. He did not make them alike. He gave the white man a heart to love peace, and the arts of a quiet life. He taught him to live in towns, to build houses, to make books, to learn all the things that would make him happy and prosperous in the way of life appointed him.

To the red man the Great Spirit gave a different character. He gave him love of the woods, of a free life of hunting and fishing, of making war with his enemies. The white man does not like to live like the Indian. It is not his nature. Neither does the Indian like to live like the white man. The Great Spirit did not make him so.

We do not wish to do anything contrary to the will of the Great Spirit. If he had made us with white skins and characters like the white man, then we would live like the white man.

We think if the Great Spirit had wished us to be like the whites, he would have made us so. We believe he would be displeased with us if we changed to try to make ourselves different from what he thought good.

If you white men had a country which was very valuable, which had always belonged to your people, and the Great Father promised should be yours forever, and men of another race came to take it away, what would your people do? Would you fight?"

This kind of talk upset Spaulding. He was so angry that he said he would listen no more and stalked out of the council tent.

After Spaulding had gone, Chief Joseph again rose to speak, saying, "The white man has been the chief obstacle in the way of the Indian civilization. The good things attempted by the government for the Indian's welfare have been turned almost completely bad by the agents employed to carry them out. The soldiers, sent for their protection, too often carried immorality and disease into their midst. The white men in the camps get our young men drunk. They steal away our daughters. They take their hearts with sweet drink and clothes. They are coyotes. The agent appointed to be our friend and counselor, business manager, and the distributor of government bounties, comes among us only to enrich himself in the shortest possible time at the cost of the Indians. They spend the largest available sum of the government money with the least visible beneficial results."

Superintendent Hale assured Joseph that he knew of the past

bad dealings and that a study was being made by the Great White Father in Washington to find the truth in these matters.

This ended that day's talks and they all went away from the council realizing they were getting nowhere. That evening, Lawyer, a chief of a small band of farming Nez Perce, and other Lapwai Chiefs were approached by Hale in secret. They were told that if they signed the treaty and got four or five other small chiefs to sign it, they would be paid $500 each year by the agent and they could assist in the distribution of goods from the government. Lawyer liked the way that sounded because he was not now powerful, but he wanted to be. He said he would try to arrange for the signing.

The next morning Mr. Spaulding was back at the council with more demands that he thought should be made of the Nez Perce, especially those at Wallowa.

"All Nez Perce should be required to attend church and live by the laws of the church, and any deviation from the law should be punished by me and the Nez Perce church leaders. In this way, we could take much power away from the chiefs and give it to the church leaders who listen to me," Mr. Spaulding said.

Chief Joseph again rose to speak.

"Our old religion seems foolish to you, but so does yours to some of my people. The Baptists, Methodists, Mormons, Presbyterians and Catholics all have a different God. Why can't we have one of our own? Why does the agent seek to take away our religion? My race is dying. Our God will soon die with us. If this new religion is not true, then what matters? I do not know what to believe. I have been a Christian for twenty-seven summers and I still do not know. If I could dream like some others say they do and visit the spirit world myself, then it would be easy to believe, but the trances do not come to me. They pass me by. If the white man takes our land, I will know that the white man's God is not my God. This much I say."

The discussions were fruitless. The Government did not want to dictate religion to the Nez Perce. It did want more land for settlers so that the territory would grow and prosper and develop wealth for the whites and power for the government. No one doubted that the land was the main issue. The treaty was ultimately drawn up so that the Nez Perce land area of the Wallowa would be cut to only one-tenth of the original size. For this the people were to get farm equipment and some white man's food and supplies.

This treaty was presented to Chief Joseph to sign. It was read to him so there would be no misunderstandings and so he knew that the white man would have a right to move into the Wallowa. Joseph stood up in astonishment. This was just what he said he did not want. They had not heard, or at least been guided by, a word he had said.

"I would never sign this treaty. This land is my father's land. It is my people's land and our children's that are not yet born. This land I would never sell. Because I do not sell it, let no white man enter to stay upon my land."

Mr. Spaulding took hold of Chief Joseph's arm saying, "Come, sign the treaty."

Joseph pushed him away hard and said, "Why do you ask me to sign away my country? It is your business to talk to us about spirit matters and not to talk to us about parting with our land."

Superintendent Hale urged Joseph to sign, but he refused.

"I will not sign your paper. You go where you please, so do I. You are not a child, I am not a child! I can think for myself.

No man can think for me. I have no other home than this. I will not give it up to any man. My people would have no home. Take away your paper. I will not touch it with my hand."

With this Joseph left the tent. Once outside he brought forth from his medicine pouch the small copy of the New Testament that he had carried since his baptism in 1836.

"Listen my people, I have carried this book with me for 27 years. I have kept it for the white man's power it should give me. I have accepted the white man's God and tried to live by some of his laws, but I am tired of the lies and deceit of the white treaty makers. I am tired of the argument among the whites about their Gods. The Great Spirit of our fathers has always remained with me. I now speak only to him in silence and go forth from the white man's religion." Saying this, Joseph tore sections of pages out of the New Testament and let them flutter to the ground in the breeze. When all the pages were gone, he mounted his horse and left the council area.

White Bird, Chief of the Nez Perce at White Goose Creek, left with Joseph. Young Looking Glass, now Chief of the Asotin band, also left. These three chiefs were the leaders of those who came to be known as the "Non-treaty Nez Perce." Indians of these three bands were semi-nomadic, living in tepees and practicing a lifestyle similar to that of the Sioux to the east. They all raised the fast, spotted horses and derived their wealth from the sale of their horses and cattle.

That night all the Nez Perce leaders held a meeting, including the Christian and non-Christian bands. This meeting lasted until early the next morning. Chief Joseph, White Bird, and Looking Glass told Lawyer and his group that this was a bad treaty and they would not sign. If Lawyer wished to sign, it would not be for them he was signing.

At the close of the meeting Joseph stood up and said, "My Chiefs, the Nez Perce nation has always been a united nation. Our people have always worked together for the good of all the people. It can no longer be so. From this day on let it be known that the people of White Bird, Looking Glass, and Joseph are separate from the rest. We do not feel the same as you do about the Great Spirit. We do not live as you do nor do we wish to. We feel no bad towards you and wish for you to feel no bad towards us. From this time forward we will say what is good for our people and you can speak for your people. Now let us go in peace as friends."

The next day Joseph, White Bird and Looking Glass stayed away from the meetings with the Superintendent of Indian Affairs. This did not sit well with Superintendent Hale. He knew he must find a way to get his treaty signed and sent to Washington. He was not in good stead with his superiors because he had not been able to get the treaty ready and signed earlier. He knew he must get it done somehow.

Without the presence of the three more powerful chiefs, Lawyer, followed by some of the other Lapwai chiefs, commenced signing the treaty. With six chief's signatures, Superintendent Hale rolled up the treaty paper and thanked the chiefs, telling them of all the goods and happiness this would bring their people. With six chiefs' signatures, the treaty paper was sent to Washington as a completed agreement of all the Nez Perce people.

As they departed, Chief Joseph counseled his sons, "When you go into council with the white man, always remember your country. Do not give it away. The white man will cheat you out of your home. I have taken no pay from the Government.

I have never sold our land. In this treaty, Lawyer acted without authority from our band. He had no right to sell the Wallowa country. That had always belonged to my father's own people, and the other bands had never disputed our right to it. No other Indians ever claimed the Wallowa."

Lawyer and his band of farmers were not injured by the treaty because it was not their land that was in question. Chief Joseph and White Bird were to lose most.

The ride home was a solemn one. Chief Joseph pondered what he might do and what the whites might do. Upon returning to the Wallowa he ordered that poles be planted around the valley which was about fifty miles wide.

"Inside is the home of my people. The white man may take the land outside. Inside this boundary all our people were born. It circles around the graves of our fathers and we will never give up these graves to any man."

In 1868, Joseph was ordered by the Secretary of the Interior to move out of the Wallowa. As a result, Joseph had a letter drawn up and sent to the Indian Commissioner in Washington telling him of the deception and informing him that Chiefs Joseph, White Bird and Looking Glass had not signed the treaty and would not sell their land nor accept any goods offered them by the agent at Lapwai.

A delegation of four Nez Perce chiefs was sent to Washington in 1868 to see if they could convince the Government that a great wrong would be done if the land was taken from the Nez Perce and given to the whites. Joseph asked to be a member of the delegation but was refused. Lawyer, Utsenmalekin, Timothy and Jason went. They were all Christian Indians who had nothing to gain by Joseph's move to Lapwai. These four were wined, dined and shown all the courtesies a diplomatic visitor might expect,

60

but little heed was paid to their weak council. They returned home with no assurance of help or understanding, but they had a good time in Washington.

Finally recognizing the problems and the potential for bloodshed if the areas controlled by these non-treaty chiefs were opened for settling, the Government quite wisely refrained from opening them up. This forestalled the settling of the area for several years. During those years, however, pressure was still being exerted on Washington by Governor Grover to open the area up.

Young Joseph had other things on his mind besides treaty problems. He was thinking of Good Woman and how he wanted her to be his wife. When they were home for a time, he told his father his desires and obtained his approval.

Joseph

He traveled back to Lapwai to ask the maiden's father for permission to marry his daughter. If he had not been the son of a great chief, his parents would have had to obtain permission for him from the parents of the girl. Then his father would have had to arrange the time of marriage and offer her father, Whisk-tasket, gifts of blankets and horses. But being a desirable suitor, Joseph himself could approach his prospective father-in-law with his request. Whisk-tasket gave his consent and waived the presents. The couple went on a two-week camp trip, then Joseph and his bride returned to the Wallowa. On their return there was a big feast.

Ollikut thought what a wonderful time this was. He hoped he, too, could find a wife to his liking and enjoy being her husband. Being one who enjoyed life and the adventures it could provide, he wondered if he would be able to find a woman who could enjoy life with him. Of all the girls he had known both at Wallowa and Lapwai, few had been exciting or interesting to him, and even fewer would have wanted to share the free life that he lived. Most of them had accepted the white man's ways liked not being an Indian squaw. Oh well, thought Ollikut, it will be sometime yet before a wife will be part of my life.

Chapter 6

THE TAMING AND TRAINING OF
HENAWIT

All summer Ollikut saw his colt often, making sure he was growing well and in good health. His excitement at the prospect of training the colt was almost more than he could control, but he knew Henawit would be much better off if he left him alone until he could be weaned. Henawit had grown in all directions. He looked better now than when he and Ollikut had first met. Ollikut thought if Henawit kept on looking better each season, he would even surpass his dreams.

That fall, the new colts were separated from their mothers and the mares were taken to another pasture several miles away so they could not hear their colts whinnying for them. A night watchman stayed with the foals to prevent them from returning to the mares. A few young geldings were mixed in with the colts as a calming influence while they adjusted to their mothers being gone. The colts had been eating grass for several months so they knew where to get their feed, but from their whinnying it was apparent they missed the comfort and security of being close to their mothers.

Henawit was no exception. He called for Sego Lily all through the night. It was not as if he had never been away from her. He had gone for half a day at a time the past month without seeing his mother. He would romp and play, racing over the plateaus with the rest of the colts. The summer had been full of new experiences, like the time he got caught in the bog and then that close call with the young wolves. Yet, now he was quite upset without his mother.

Early the next day, Ollikut went out to the meadow where the colts were being held. He and the night rider pushed the colts into the breaking corrals so they could be caught and broke to lead.

This was the first time Henawit had been in an enclosure. He bumped the poles quite hard and felt the pain. Sticking his head between two poles he lunged forward, trying to squeeze through, but they were just too strong.

Ollikut knew the colt would be a handful. He decided to work on him first while he was fresh and at his peak strength. After working with two or three colts, he would be more tired and more apt to lose his temper.

Picking up his rope, he walked into the corral. Henawit seemed to recognize him from his many visits. They had become what you might call nodding acquaintances. When Ollikut made his visits to the meadow in the summer, Henawit would always come out of the band toward him and shake his head up and down, nodding, trying to see if Ollikut would scare. This time was no exception. Henawit came forward as usual. If only I could walk up to him, Ollikut thought. Holding the rope down to his side, he slowly walked towards the colt. One step, then another and yet another. He was now within reach of Henawit. The colt had observed every movement Ollikut made. Ollikut wondered if he remembered the time before when he got this close then grabbed for his neck. Henawit turned and worked his way back through the other colts not wanting Ollikut that close.

Realizing that he would not be able to walk up to the colt, Ollikut decided to rope him. Building a loop in his rawhide rope he walked as close as he could to the colt, then with one swing around his head the rope sailed out and landed softly around the neck of Henawit. Fear seemed to shoot through Henawit's body. As the rope tightened, it became hard for him to breathe. Henawit hung back and fought the end of the rope with all his strength. Getting light-headed, he stopped fighting and braced four feet so as not to fall down.

Only a big, young man like Ollikut, could match such a colt. But Ollikut, too, showed signs of wear. His hands had rope burns on them and he was dusty inside and out since the colt had drug him through the dry, dusty corral.

Ollikut could see the colt was getting dizzy. He knew if he pulled any more the colt would pass out, but if he loosened up now he would regain his air and fight more. The timing had to be just right. Waiting a few more seconds until the colt started to get wobbly, Ollikut walked up the rope and made a loop to put around the colt's nose with part of the rope that was around the colt's neck. This was done before Henawit even knew he was there. Within seconds Henawit had regained his air and his head cleared.

With the loop over the nose, Ollikut could control the colt's head and make him face him. Each time Henawit turned to go back to the colts, Ollikut gave a pull on the rope which brought the colt right around to face him. The rope was tight. It hurt over his nose and behind his ears. Ollikut knew it hurt, but he also knew that Henawit had to learn to respect that rope. He had to learn not to pull on it. The only way for him to learn was to have it hurt a little.

Ollikut had seen too many horses that had not learned this lesson and could not be tied or even led. They were of no value. By being too easy on them as colts, their owners lost the horse's usefulness. Henawit had to learn and remember this first vital lesson. Ollikut knew it would take much time and repetition. Ollikut's father had taught him that a horse learns to understand and fulfill the trainer's desires only through patience and repetition so that was what he had to do.

Ollikut worked his way up the rope, and as he did, Henawit kept trying to turn away. With a firm tug on the rope Ollikut was able to make the colt face him. Rubbing the colt on the neck he worked up the rope and loosened the pressure over his nose and behind his ears. This was a relief for the colt, but he didn't like Ollikut so close. Turning, he pulled away trying to get back to the other colts. With a firm tug, Ollikut again tightened the rope over the nose and behind the ears. This brought the colt around to face him again. Once more Ollikut walked up the rope and loosened the pressure.

This went on for more than half an hour. Henawit found to prevent the rope pressure, he must turn towards Ollikut. Once Ollikut got this through to the colt, he then started pulling, from side to side on the rope. At first Henawit fought back at these pulls. Soon he found by giving to the pull, the pressure lessened.

Realizing Henawit had learned what he wanted, Ollikut decided it was time to work on another colt and let Henawit stand and think about this. Working his way to the colt's head, he slipped the noose off his nose and tightened it around the neck. Next, he slipped on a headstall with a rawhide-braided nose band. Attached to this was a short rope. Ollikut led the colt out of the corral with the help of someone behind him shooing him along. Finding a strong young tree, Ollikut tied

Henawit's rope about five feet high.

Henawit didn't like this, so he hung back and pulled. The tree bent a little with the pull but held firm. Henawit felt the rawhide bite into his nose and could feel the pressure behind his ears. This was very uncomfortable. Jumping forward, he found the pressure eased and the rawhide stopped biting his nose. One try was not enough for Henawit, though. He pulled back, turned, and went around the tree one way, then the other. He finally realized he could move all he wanted as long as he stopped when the rope became tight.

Ollikut left the colt tied for the rest of the morning. It was a warm day and Henawit was hot and thirsty. The colt's getting thirsty was part of Ollikut's plan. When he untied Henawit and started toward the creek, the colt was coming up behind at a fast walk. Henawit did not realize that Ollikut was leading him. The colt was heading to the creek for a drink, and Ollikut was just going the same way.

Returning to the corral was a different matter. Henawit did not want to return to the corral. Planting all four feet, he meant to stand his ground. Rather than fight him, Ollikut took his rope and put a loop over the colt's rump. Giving a tug with the lead rope and getting no response, he would jerk the butt rope and Henawit would jump forward. Henawit couldn't quite figure this out. There was no one in back of him, yet he kept getting jerked in the back of the legs. He soon learned that by walking up when he was led, the jerking stopped.

As Ollikut slid the headstall off the colt's head, he rubbed him under the chin and behind the ears. This really felt good but, even so, Henawit still wanted to leave Ollikut and get back to the colts.

The past two days had been quite eventful for Henawit, not pleasant but eventful. The next few days proved even more interesting. Ollikut was up early each morning working with the colts. This was not easy work, but it was enjoyable because he could see the results of what he was doing. All the colts were coming along well and gentling down considerably.

Every once in a while Henawit would try to paw Ollikut when he went to reach for a front leg. This had to stop. Ollikut made a pair of hobbles out of rawhide and put them on the colt. This was anything but easy to accomplish. Only with the assistance of another colt breaker could Ollikut get both of Henawit's feet hobbled at once.

Henawit didn't know what to make of this. He reared up, pawing the air, but the feet were tied so they had only about six inches between them and that was all the give he could get. Coming back down to the ground, he found walking even harder. As soon as he had quit fighting, Ollikut started rubbing the tendons in the back of his lower legs. It wasn't really so bad and, before long, the hobbles came off.

Soon Henawit stood at ease when Ollikut rubbed him and picked up his feet. He began to trust Ollikut enough that he didn't even try to kick him when he walked behind him. A bond of understanding and respect was forming that would last for many moons, through good and bad times.

Chapter 7
A CHANGE IN RELIGION

Not long after Chief Joseph had torn up his New Testament a stranger appeared in camp. His name was Smohalla. He proclaimed himself a medicine man. This medicine man brought with him a new religion with a little Catholic, Mormon, and Protestant doctrine thrown in. At the heart of this new religion was the superiority of the Indian and disdain for the whites. The treaty Indians called the medicine man Too'at or Dreamer. The elders at Lapwai considered him to be a charlatan with bad dreams. They told their people to stay away from his meetings. Nothing good could come from listening to him.

Smohalla was a small man with a large head and humped shoulders. He looked every bit the part of an odd wizard of a medicine man. His speeches, at times, attained oratorical eloquence that could hold his listeners, Indians and whites alike, spellbound. Even whites who did not understand the language were amazed at his voice control and effective inflections accompanied by dramatic gestures. He had learned the white man's language, too. His persuasive manner of speaking was enough to captivate his audience for hours in either language.

Chief Joseph was looking for a religion he could understand. He wanted no more to do with the white man's religions. He had even begun to question the old Indian beliefs. As a believer in a great power that came from above and made a place for the Indians, he needed a religion that would give him a basis for believing in the hereafter.

Smohalla was easily accepted as a medicine man. Old Looking Glass had told of him riding in a battle against a raiding party of Blackfeet a number of years ago. Smohalla had been shot and killed near the big river, Columbia. Looking Glass had seen him lying there dead. After the fight the Nez Perce warriors returned to collect their dead and wounded, but Smohalla had vanished.

Actually, after being shot with a Blackfoot arrow, Smohalla had fallen and lay unconscious for sometime. Coming to and realizing the Blackfeet were all around, he slipped into the river holding onto a big log that floated downstream. A friendly white farmer found him and nursed him back to health. Instead of returning home, Smohalla continued down the Columbia. He went to Seattle where he spent some time in work and thought, learning to read and write in English. From there he traveled to San Francisco. After a few years in the South, he started home by way of the Great Basin and Salt Lake City. He spent some time with the Mormons. After being partially converted, he returned home. He had become wise in the ways of the white man and had learned much about religion and missionary work. From this he built his plan. He would tell the Nez Perce people he had died and passed into the world beyond and that he had walked with the Great Spirit and many of the Chiefs that had died. The Great Spirit then permitted him to return to teach and guide the Nez Perce people.

The Dreamer related to the non-treaty Nez Perce how the Great Spirit had sent him to teach them things that the Great Spirit wanted them to understand. The first principle he was to explain was that all other religions were wrong. One had the power of the Great Spirit. Smohalla had been given back his life so he could bring these truths and powers to the Nez Perce people.

The Dreamer also claimed that the Great Spirit talked to him whenever he asked, as if two friends talked. He said that he had been sent to help the Nez Perce keep the white men out of the Indian's land. He reported that while in the world beyond he talked with the Great Spirit and was told that other lands were prepared for the white man and that he was very displeased that they had left these lands to take what was not given to them.

In a meeting at Wallowa, the Dreamer said, "Once, many moons ago the Great Spirit had come to the Nez Perce land to talk to the people. He told them he would send one of his children to guide them when the time came that they were in need of guidance and were worthy of it."

Smohalla reported that he was the one. He explained the creation.

"The Great Spirit created the Indian country and it was like he spread out a big blanket. Then the Great Spirit created fish in the river, put deer in the mountains and made physical laws through which come increases of fish and game. Next, he gave the Indians life. We were created here in this country, truly and honestly, and that was when the river started to run. We awakened and as soon as we saw the game and fish we knew that they were made for us. For the women, he made roots and berries to gather, and the Indians grew and multiplied as a people."

"When we were created we were given this land to live on, and from that time these were our rights. This is all true. We had the fish before the missionaries came, before the white man came. We were put here by the Great Spirit and given these rights farther back than our grandfather could remember. This was the food on which we lived. Our mothers gathered berries. Our fathers fished and killed the deer, but only what they needed. These words are that of the Great Spirit and they are true. It matters not how long we live. We cannot change these thoughts. Our strength is from the spotted horse. Our blood is from the meat of the animals, the fish, from the roots and the berries. The fish and game are the essence of our life. We were put here by the Great Spirit. We had no cattle, no hogs, no grain, only berries, roots, fish and wild game. We have always taken care of what the Great Spirit gave us. We have helped it grow and continue."

Pausing, as if going into a trance, Smohalla said:

"The Great Spirit came to me saying: Because I am the Maker of heavens and earth, the trees, lakes, rivers, and all else. Because I am the Maker of all mankind and because I love you, you must do my will. The land on which you live I have made for you and not for others. Why do you suffer the white man to dwell among you? My children, you have forgotten the customs and traditions of your forefathers. Why do some of you clothe yourselves in white man's clothes? You should wear skins, as our fathers did, use bows and arrows and stone-pointed lances, which they used. You have bought guns, knives, kettles and blankets from the white man until you can no longer do without them. What is worse, you have drunk the poison firewater, which turns you into fools. Fling all these things away. Live as your wise forefathers did before you." Smohalla again paused before continuing.

"See I told you we should return to wearing skins and huntng with the bow. We have become soft living the white man ways in much that we do," Ollikut told Joseph.

"Why should we give up the things the white man has that makes our lives better. We don't go hungry because the rifle shoots straighter and faster than our bows so we eat better. When there is little game we have the cattle we raise to eat," Joseph replied back.

"Since we received the spotted horse we have hunted buffalo with the Sioux. The new treaty does not permit the Nez Perce to leave the Wallowa to hunt to the east. I want to hunt buffalo every summer for the rest of my life. I will not return to the mission school at Lapwai," Ollikut asserted.

The Dreamer started to speak again.

"Some of our chiefs claim that the land belongs to them. That is not what the Great Spirit told me. He told me that the land belongs to him, no people own the land. He said you were not to forget to tell this to the white men when you meet in council. If council fails, you are to hold the land that is his with every breath within your body. This was the land his childrens' bones have been buried in from the first day. It should not be defiled by the whites."

Even some treaty Nez Perce at Lapwai found good in the ideas of the Dreamer, especially when he spoke on his work ethic.

For Smohalla said, "Young men should never work, for those that work cannot dream. Wisdom comes to us in dreams. You ask me to plow the ground. Shall I take a knife and tear my mother's bosom? You ask me to dig for stone. Shall I dig under her skin for her bones? You ask me to cut grass and make hay and sell it and be rich like white men. But how dare I cut off my mother's hair?"

Many of the young men at Lapwai were becoming tired of farming. They had been looked down on by the non-treaty Indians for their dress and woman's work they were doing. These young men hungered for the fast horses they saw their non-treaty brothers riding while they drove a slow plodding team.

The white men treated them no better for having followed the white man's ways. They were always being lied to and promised goods in return for labor or produce from their farms. When they did not get fair payment there was little they could do but tell the agent about it. If he was in the right mood he would write a letter to his superiors. Little, if any, results ever came of a complaint. Therefore, it was easy to want to follow the Dreamer.

Young Joseph clung to the white man's teaching of religion quite strongly, even though he did not go to their meetings anymore.

"Ollikut, you must not believe in the Dreamer's teachings. He preaches violence when wronged. We believe in peace, not violence. The white men will see that the new treaty is unfair to us. They will change the treaty."

"But Joseph, you want peace at most any price. I know you are not a violent man, but there is a point at which you must fight or lose your pride as a man."

Ollikut had found the Dreamer in tune with his own thoughts. This was his land to live on and use until he died. He was determined to keep the white man out. If it took violence, so be it!

Ollikut attended many meetings where the Dreamer talked. His father went also. They both felt very close to the Wallowa. Old Joseph realized that Ollikut, not Joseph, was the natural leader of the young men. He was a man's man who could never ask another to do what he would not do himself.

Converts flocked to the Dreamer. They came mainly from the non-treaty Indians, but as time passed a large number of disillusioned young treaty Indians also joined his ranks. Young Joseph held steadfast to the Protestant religion that the Spauldings had taught them.

Chapter 8
RIDING AT LAST

Another winter had come and gone. Ollikut was anxious to start working with Henawit now that spring had turned the grass green and the trees were in full leaf.

Ollikut felt the time would come when he and Henawit would live the dream he had in his quest. The Dreamer foretold that there would be rumors of wars and then real wars to hold the land of their fathers.

The whites as well as the Nez Perce at Lapawi looked with disdain and distrust at Ollikut every time he rode into Lapwai on a fine spotted horse of his fathers. He could feel this dislike from the older Indians. The young men looked more with hope and desire to be able to live such a life and to have such a fine horse.

Ollikut remembered his dream. Henawit was there. He saw Henawit as a spirit horse carrying him from one battle to another. He counted many battles. How could this dream be true? The Nez Perce tribe had been at peace as long as his father and his father before could remember. Yet, maybe the Dreamer was right. Maybe there would be war.

For over two and a half years Ollikut worked off and on with Henawit teaching him to lead, to stand ground-tied, and in general, to be gentle and quiet. Some months Henawit was left free to run and play in the hills and learn to follow trails and jump logs as a wild one.

While working with Henawit, Ollikut had taught him a number of voice commands such as whoa, back, walk, and trot. A kissing sound meant to gallop. At the end of a long rope Henawit would move in a circle around Ollikut. As Ollikut called out a command, the colt would react to it. This had taken many hours of patient work. Through this work they became aware of each other's moods and feelings. When Ollikut was feeling happy and boisterous, Henawit would jump and buck, kicking up his heels. But some days it seemed best just to do as Ollikut said with no playing around. Henawit had his good and bad days, too, and acted accordingly. Each of them realized that they wanted each other's friendship and trust. With this realization came the feeling of oneness that few men and animals ever know.

The Nez Perce were the only Indians of that time to practice gelding poorer quality stud horses. They were also the most advanced in horse breeding and training. That was why their horses were so sought after by the Indians and whites.

Henawit was not used for breeding at this early age. He was pastured with the older geldings. These older horses would not take any nonsense from him and he learned to control his actions in the herd and around the mares. Now it was time to go one step further. The big three-year-old colt had to learn to carry a man's weight. He had to learn how to take commands from the rider's legs and body.

Henawit was already accustomed to the rawhide nose band. This was what Ollikut intended to use to teach him to guide. Some of the Nez Perce were using the steel bit of the white man to break and ride their horses, but Ollikut preferred the old way. This way Henawit already would know about being pulled around. Being on him would not make much difference to the pull. He should still give to the pressure.

Over the past year, Ollikut had worked so much with the colt that putting the pad and saddle on was no problem at all. The pad made by Navajo Indians was of woven wool. He also had a saddle made by the Sioux. The saddle was carved out of wood, then covered with wet rawhide. His father had traded for it while on a buffalo hunt with the Sioux. Ollikut used a soft tanned deer hide to cover the saddle and then tied everything in place with a strap around the deer hide and under the horse's belly.

After the saddle was in place, Ollikut tied the left rein short to Henawit's tail, so that the colt would have to turn in a left circle when he moved. After a short time, Ollikut tied the right rein to the tail and let Henawit walk in a right circle for a while. None of this upset Henawit because he was used to the pull of the rawhide nose band and gave to it when it started causing pressure.

There was only one thing left to do and that was to get on. This was the day he had been waiting for since he had mated Sego Lily with Le Bleu. Just so there wouldn't be a problem, Ollikut hobbled Henawit while he got on and off a few times. At the first mounting the big colt wanted to jump, but Ollikut spent sometime making sure Henawit had no reason to be afraid of him mounting and dismounting. A horse must stand quiet while being mounted, even in battle. If he didn't, it could mean the rider's life. Ollikut knew Henawit would be great in battle. His dream had shown him that.

After Ollikut felt sure the colt was at ease, he took the hobbles off and then got on and off Henawit's back a couple more times. Henawit was not really sure the hobbles were off and so he held his feet in place.

Feeling more confident now that Henawit would stay quiet during mounting and dismounting, Ollikut kicked him in the ribs lightly to get him to move off. Nothing happened, for

Henawit still thought he had hobbles on. Ollikut took the reins and slapped him on the rump. The colt jumped with both legs, thinking they were tied together, but found them free. The jump rocked Ollikut in the saddle, pulling on the belly strap. This upset Henawit and he started to jump. He knew nothing about bucking, other than just the jumping and kicking he had done in the meadow; but even this made it tough for Ollikut to stay on such a big powerful colt. Ollikut had ridden a number of bucking horses while breaking horses for his father. He had also ridden some older spoiled horses that knew how to buck, so he had had practice at such riding. Until now the colt had been no match for his skill.

This time something strange happened. The colt went up high, hit the ground hard and sucked back. All at once Ollikut could feel the ground coming up at him fast. The saddle was still between his legs so he knew the colt was coming over on him. He dove to the side as he hit, just glancing back to see which way Henawit was falling. Instead of Henawit, there was just the blanket falling through the air. Henawit just stood back in disbelief. The saddle had slipped over the colt's shoulders and head, falling to the ground with Ollikut still in it.

Gathering himself to a sitting position, Ollikut broke into laughter, for Henawit was still standing spraddle-legged and wide-eyed, with both ears intensely pointed towards the pile of saddle and man. The accident had scared him as much as it had Ollikut.

Ollikut had taken falls before, but when a horse came over on him, he never got up laughing. This time he didn't even have a scratch. Taking his time he wiped the dirt from his face, brushed himself off and began picking up the saddle and blankets. Then he placed them on Henawit's quivering back. Hobbling him again, Ollikut repeated the mounting and dismounting until both he and Henawit began to relax again. This time he tightened the cinch more, took off the hobbles and then turned the horse so he could feel his feet were free. Then Ollikut mounted taking a deep seat and tight hold, but the big colt just trotted around the breaking corral. This time there was no jumping, bucking, or running, just a walk and slow trot. After a few minutes of this Ollikut said, "Whoa," then dismounted and pulled off the saddle and headstall.

Henawit was loose for another night. He seemed to be able to carry the weight easily. Ollikut could tell he wasn't afraid of being ridden. Ollikut wondered if Henawit had found the day as interesting as he had. The fall was not in Ollikut's plans, but it was his fault for not tightening the cinch before he mounted for the first ride. Next time he would be more careful.

A week passed with Ollikut riding some each day. Henawit was getting to know what was expected. He especially seemed to enjoy going out in the meadow and over the hills.

Every time Ollikut turned him, he would pull on the rein in the direction that he wanted him to go, laying the other rein against his neck. With his leg he would open his leg pressure on the side he wanted to go and squeeze with the other leg. In this way Henawit learned to turn on Ollikut's leg commands. In battle, Ollikut could guide Henawit with his legs while he shot arrows or a rifle when he needed both hands. In his dream Henawit had moved to his leg commands dodging the enemy's arrows and bullets. Ollikut knew Henawit was a spirit horse.

One day while riding in the hills, Ollikut saw a young deer and decided to give chase. Henawit was jumping over brush and rocks as they scrambled up the hill. It felt as if he had wings. They reached the top of the ridge and entered an area with a sprinkling of pines. As Ollikut guided Henawit down a slope, they came to a spot where the trail forked with a big tree in the middle. Ollikut guided the colt to the left, leaning lightly to that side. Seeing a gopher hole on that side, Henawit went to the right, but Ollikut had already committed himself to the left. This placed Ollikut in the same place as the tree, and the tree was not about to move.

Some moments later, Ollikut rolled over and moaned. Looking up, he met the inquisitive eyes of Henawit. He knew the colt had meant no harm but was just trying not to step in the gopher hole. His years of running loose had taught him to watch for holes. This did not help the pain in Ollikut's head and chest. He was very pleased that Henawit had not run home. Rather, he had remained ground tied when the reins dropped. Pulling himself up against the tree, Ollikut stood as straight as he could. Every time he took a breath, the pain increased. He knew his ribs were cracked or possibly broken. With painful motion Ollikut crawled up on Henawit's back and let the colt walk very slowly back to camp.

The colt got a two week rest because of the accident. It was nice for Henawit to romp and play in the meadow.

As soon as Ollikut could ride without too much pain, he was back working on the colt. Hour after hour he rode through the hills. Every time he turned Henawit with the reins, he would leg cue him, too. The leg pressure came to be Henawit's main cue. Ollikut would practice running through a thin pine tree stand using just his legs to maneuver around the trees. Henawit soon learned to react to Ollikut's cue and not to think for himself as to which side of the tree to go. Once he had learned this, Ollikut felt much more at ease when they were in timber.

A buffalo hunt was the real test of a horse's speed and handling ability. Ollikut wanted to use Henawit for a buffalo hunt and knew he must be well trained so that he would approach the buffalo and not be scared. Some horses seeing buffalo for the first time would not get closer than twenty feet, if even that. Their smell was new and different to the horse. They looked peculiar compared to the cows the colts had ranged with. Ollikut knew he had to work with Henawit many more times if he was to perform as he should during the hunt.

For a number of days Ollikut rode Henawit through the cow herds. He would scare the cattle until they would slowly run off. Once they started running, he would ride Henawit along side one until he could put his foot on its hip. Soon Henawit learned what was wanted and would move in and hold his position as Ollikut put his foot on the cow two or three times. Henawit was always rewarded with a fond pat on his great spirit horse neck at the end of a chase.

The training was coming along, but it was far from over. Ollikut knew Henawit was fast enough to catch the buffalo, but would he get close to one? To be sure that he would perform properly, Ollikut took a buffalo hide and had two of his friends help him catch a steer and tie the hide to it. The steer was not too happy about the situation, so as soon as they had it tied in place Ollikut got on Henawit and told his friends to turn the steer loose. The steer ran and bucked and kicked. Between his antics and the shaggy hide he looked very strange and non-cowlike. Henawit wanted nothing to do with him. He would get up to within about fifteen feet of the steer then slack off or cut to the side. Ollikut anticipated his reaction and kept reassuring him and pushing him on. The steer soon tired and slowed to a trot. Henawit came within ten feet of him, but that was the best he would do. Then the steer stopped. Henawit moved in closer and smelled the hide. His nose flared and he snorted and blew. He was not accustomed to the smell. Ollikut knew that the colt needed to get use to the smell and sight of the buffalo so he drove the steer to the breaking corral and, once inside, he turned Henawit loose with the steer disguised as a buffalo.

The next day he turned the steer with the buffalo hide tied on him out and rode after him. Henawit stepped right up in the proper position with only a little extra encouragement. This was what Ollikut had hoped for but couldn't count on. He continued chasing buffalo hide-covered steers a little while each day for a couple of weeks until Henawit ran to them as easily as he had plain steers. Ollikut knew this training might not be well enough remembered by Henawit if it was not reviewed once in a while before he and his father went to Montana the next summer to hunt with Chief Crazy Horse of the Sioux. Joseph had accepted his invitation by messengers the month before. By then Henawit would be older and stronger, and Ollikut was determined that Henawit would be finely trained for the hunt along with having more desire to race, too.

During this time, the Dreamer was gaining more and more converts, many of whom were very rebellious and warlike towards the whites. This drew the treaty and non-treaty Nez Perce further apart.

Old Chief Joseph cautioned the Dreamer that his way would surely lead to war. There was no good that could come of war and Joseph knew it. The whites were now too many and the Indians too few for war. He also knew that if the situation worsened he would rather die in war than tolerate being imprisoned on a reservation. All his life he had lived the free life. He knew it would kill his spirit to live on twenty acres and drive a team.

The Dreamer had taken an interest in Ollikut. He saw him at many of the meetings and found that he was Chief Joseph's son.

Even though the Dreamer was quite persuasive, Ollikut was not totally convinced his religion was the right one either. Ollikut was a deep thinker, as was Young Joseph, only he was much more questioning than Joseph.

The Dreamer said that he spoke to the Great Spirit and the Great Spirit spoke back to him. Ollikut had not heard of the Great Spirit talking to anyone else. Yet, he believed what the Dreamer said about what the Spirit said.

"Joseph, do you think the Great Spirit could talk to you like we are talking?" Ollikut asked.

"I believe you can talk to the Great Spirit and you can see your question answered in your dreams. You just have to listen to your dreams rather than listening to the Dreamer. The Spirit won't tell him what he wants only you to know."

"I am going to ask the Great Spirit about my dream. I have told no one and see if he sends me a message. We will talk more about this."

Ollikut stayed away from the meetings for a couple of weeks. One day the Dreamer approached Ollikut saying, "Why have you missed my meetings? You did come often. Now you don't come at all."

"I have been searching my mind for answers. I have asked the Great Spirit to interpret my dreams that I received on my quest. I am waiting for an answer but have not received it yet."

"Tell me your dream and I will tell you what it means."

"No, my dream is only for me to know. I must find the meaning in my own way and in the Great Spirit's way."

"Don't you believe what I have told you about the white man's evil and that this land was given to the Indians to care for and live on?"

"I believe this but I know that my brother speaks true when he tells me not to listen to your approval of violence against the whites."

"One day you will see the whites come to take your people's land. There will be killings and you will find yourself leading your brother out of danger just to find more danger the next day. I have seen the dreams and am sure you have seen the dreams, too."

Ollikut put these thoughts out of his head as he prepared for more adventure. The Indian agent had not been able to get the Army to enforce the new treaty. The non-treaty Indians were still living under the rules of the 1855 treaty. Everyone wondered when the new treaty would be enforced.

Chapter 9

THE BUFFALO HUNT

Excitement had been running high all spring. The rumor of a buffalo hunt had been passed around and everyone knew the new treaty prohibited the Nez Perce from traveling to the buffalo country. For this reason, the secret had not been advertised. Now it was time to prepare for the journey. They could no longer hide their plans for the trip. The news traveled fast.

Chief Joseph was summoned into the Indian agent's office. He arrived a day late for the meeting. He did not want the agent thinking he could order him to come or go.

"You can not leave the Wallowa. You know the new treaty prohibits you from going to the buffalo country to hunt. You must stay on the reservation."

"We Wallowa Nez Perce are not bound by the new treaty. We never signed the new treaty and we never took any of your gifts for the land. We can come and go as we choose. You can not force us to do anything we wish not to do. If you call the soldiers, there will be killings on both sides."

Chief Joseph departed with the agent hollering threats at him as he left. There was a big chance that he would send soldiers to block the trail out of the Wallowa Valley. Still, Joseph was dertermined to hunt the buffalo.

The time finally came to travel to the buffalo grounds to the east. Now Ollikut could see if his long periods of training Henawit had been worthwhile. Excitement ran high in Ollikut's head. He had not been on a buffalo hunt before. He had heard so many stories about the hunts that he could see in his mind just what they would be like.

The night before they were to leave, Ollikut heard the criers riding through camp crying out the instructions from the leaders. They told everyone going to get things packed for an early departure in the morning.

Sleep came slowly for Ollikut that night. All he could think of was riding alongside a big bull and shooting an arrow straight into its heart. As he slept, he dreamed of racing up to buffalo after buffalo. By the end of the sleep, he must have killed over fifty buffalo.

Upon rising, Ollikut caught Henawit and saddled him. He packed all the belongings he would need on a pack horse. Extra horses were put in one group for the trip. Ollikut picked two of his next best mounts and took them to the holding area. Now he was ready.

Not all the people were going. The old and weak stayed in the Wallowa and took care of the homeland and the livestock while the hunters and their families were away.

As the party readied for the hunt, Ollikut went around and helped those who were having problems. He was strong and could lift and hold large packs while they were strapped in place.

Soon all were ready and everyone waited for the criers to indicate the start of the trip. The criers rode around telling the people to get in their place. Scouts went out first, then came Chief Joseph followed by some elders. The warriors rode next in line. Then came the hunters who had not been to battle yet. Ollikut and Joseph rode at the head of this group. After these men came the women riding and leading the loaded packhorses. The climb up out of the valley to the plateau was too steep and narrow in places to use pony drags like the Sioux. All their goods were packed on the backs of the pack horses.

Chief Joseph had warned the warriors that there might be trouble from the soldiers. They were to be prepared to move up in front if the scouts saw any soldiers.

The people were happy. Ollikut could hear singing up and down the long line of riders. Once more he thought of the friends he had made at Lapwai and knew they would never know this free and happy feeling as he rode his spirit horse, Henawit, toward the buffalo country. If he were forced to live on twenty acres and to farm, he knew he would surely die in his heart.

Of all the white man's rules, not going to the buffalo grounds was the most cruel of all. It took the last great adventure out of the lives of those who obeyed. He prayed to the Great Spirit that his father would never ask him to obey that rule. He wanted to go on many buffalo hunts, to see new country and meet new people, to learn of the ways of these people and to be considered a friend, if they would have it so.

Life had been very good to him, he thought as they rode through the beautiful mountains. He had learned to hunt and ride. His father and uncle had shown him how to train horses and he had enjoyed his work. Now he had twenty of his own horses. His best mares had been bred to Henawit. By now he had some colts from Henawit. As Ollikut had expected, he had put size, conformation and color into all of the foals. This was the true sign of a useful sire.

By trading off some low-quality stock he had taken for breaking other horses, Ollikut had obtained robes, moccasins, leggings and other finery. He also had some gold in his cache. With this he could buy from the white man the goods of their making he desired. How could he say life had been less than good to him? He could not.

The sun was straight overhead when they reached the first rocky pass in the mountains. The going was slow and the horses had to be stopped often for a rest. Henawit, however, hardly had a sweat. He had a lot of endurance and heart. Getting him tired would take more than this.

While they stopped to rest, the boys looked for grouse to shoot with their arrows and the girls picked flowers or sometimes berries when they could be found.

At this pass, the scouts hurried back to the caravan.

"Soldiers! Soldiers!" they shouted.

The column halted while the warriors rode past the elders. Ollikut and Joseph rode up with the warriors. There were thirty-four warriors plus Ollikut and Joseph all armed with rifles.

Chief Joseph led the warriors to the top of the pass where the soldiers were stationed.

"We request to pass," Chief Joseph said.

"We have orders to turn you back," the Captain said.

"You see I have many warriors and more are in the trees on each side of you. If you persist, there will be many dead on your side and my side as well. You would think well to move away so we can pass. We mean to harm no one but we will fight if our path is restricted."

The Captain looked to each side and could see there were warriors close by. He knew he wasn't in a good position to fight.

"It looks like you have the advantage today. I won't be so naive the next time we meet," the Captain said and moved off the trail.

Chief Joseph was pleased there was no fighting. Ollikut knew that fighting with the women there would be very dangerous.

Each day they would travel about twenty or more miles. After the ninth day of travel the scouts returned with the news that Chief Crazy Horse of the Bad Face Sioux was within a two-hour ride of them. Chief Crazy Horse had sent a messenger to Chief Joseph that spring inviting him to hunt with the Sioux in the fall. Crazy Horse was a brave warrior who had counted many coups, so many that when he cornered an enemy he no longer counted coup. He permitted someone else to take that honor. Ollikut was anxious to see this great, big, powerful chief and warrior.

Excitement ran through the travelers with the news of the Sioux so close. In less than two hours they came in sight of Crazy Horse's camp. It did not take long for them to set up camp a short distance from Crazy Horse's and start the evening meal.

To show their pleasure at the Nez Perce's arrival, a party of Sioux brought over a whole buffalo. All the women came and cut what they wanted from the carcass. This was a treat because the buffalo was about as tasty a meat as could be found, better even than the cattle they raised in the Wallowa.

This was one of the problems. The white men could see no reason for the non-treaty Nez Perce going on buffalo hunts when they had more than ample cattle for their meat needs. It would have seemed much more logical, to the whites, if the treaty Indians on the small farms wanted to go to get meat for the winter.

To the people of Chief Joseph's band, however, it was a vacation, a trip of happiness. Buffalo was a delicacy to them for they could have beef anytime. The fat, young buffalo cows were tender and easier for the old people to chew and digest than the beef. If the hunt was good, all the extra horses would be loaded with meat to carry back for the whole band.

Crazy Horse invited Chief Joseph and his two sons to eat with him. This was just what Ollikut had been waiting for, a chance to meet the great Chief Crazy Horse. Ollikut was expecting to see a man at least as big as he from all the great deeds he had heard. To his surprise Crazy Horse was a small, slender man, yet very strong. His face was lean and dark with a scar here and there. These were his battle marks. His hair was not as dark as most of the Sioux but rather a bit brown. He wore his hair in braids hanging past his shoulders.

It seemed strange to Ollikut that such a small man could have done all the deeds he had heard about. It must be true, though, for everyone knew the stories.

The meal was very good. The buffalo had been cooked just the way Ollikut liked it, crisp on the outside and pink on the inside. The talk was also good. Crazy Horse told of the last hunt and how plentiful the buffalo were this year. Chief Joseph told of the treaty problems and asked Crazy Horse for his advice. Being a fighter and not a talker, Crazy Horse advised war before a reservation. He said it would be better to die in battle than grow old and die hungry and tired on a reservation.

"Your bones should be buried on the land of your fathers, the land you love, not on some distant, unhappy reservation," Crazy Horse said.

After much talk and smoking of the pipe, the party broke up. Chief Joseph and his sons walked back to their tepee. On the way back Ollikut asked, "Father, what made this small man such a brave warrior?"

"It is an Indian belief that the youngest son in a family always had to compete with his older brothers who have already had more years to gain honor; the youngest must be especially brave and daring from the very first and not fear anything. He worked hard to be called more brave than his older brothers. It is said Crazy Horse realized this so he gathered the youngest sons of many families. They were daring fighters. With him to lead, not fearing death himself, they had accomplished many brave deeds,"Chief Joseph said.

This seemed quite logical to Ollikut once he thought a bit about it. He had tried harder to be a man because his brother Joseph was older and was already counted as a man. Ollikut practiced hunting, shooting and riding more because he wanted to be the best. Not just as good, but the best in the Wallowa. Maybe that was why he and Henawit got along so well, because Henawit seemed to have a similar drive. They were spirit brothers to the end.

Sleep came hard again this night because Ollikut knew they would hunt the buffalo the old way with just a bow and arrow. Would he be up to the hunt and would Henawit respond to his every command? Would he have honor in his first hunt or would he not find a vital organ with his arrow? Finally he fell into a deep sleep after a long exciting day.

Scouts were sent out at the break of day to look for a herd of buffalo to attack. It was just after breakfast when the crier shouted.

"They are back. The scouts have returned."

The scouts rode up to Crazy Horse's tepee and dismounted. Joseph and his sons were there waiting for the news. The scouts had found a large herd moving slowly south within five miles of the camp. With this news everyone mounted up. This was a big hunting party with the Sioux and Nez Perce combined. Riding on a trot, then a lope and back to a trot, the five miles passed quite rapidly. Soon they could see the dust and hear the rumbling of the buffalo herd moving.

Stopping on a bluff overlooking the plains they could see a herd of possibly a thousand buffalo. It looked like a cattle drive. They were not grazing, but moving in a herd to other feed grounds. They looked much bigger to Ollikut than he had pictured them. When he tied the buffalo robe on the steer and chased it, he was much higher than what it looked like he would be to these live buffalo. That meant he would need to reconsider what aim should be taken to hit a vital organ for the kill.

As they watched the herd, their ponies rested for the run to the buffalo. Ollikut looked at Henawit and saw he was hardly sweating. He knew he could do a fine job today.

As they watched from the bluff, Ollikut saw an old bull surrounded by three younger, smaller bulls. The old bull was pawing the ground and digging up clumps of sod with his horns. One young bull stepped forward and bellowed, then started pawing the ground. At about the same instant the two bulls made a run at each other, colliding with a solid blow. They stepped off a couple steps then hit again. The old bull slipped off to the side where he began hooking his horn in the side and stomach of the young bull. It did not take many thrusts to break a hole in the side of his rival. It went through the hide and into the intestines. A couple more hooks and the young bull was almost disemboweled and dying.

Another young bull immediately gave a bellow and pawed the ground in defiance of the old bull. Only having a few cuts from the first battle, the old bull accepted the challenge and the fight began. This fight ended similar to the first except for the old bull having a few more spots of blood on his shoulders and stomach.

The third young bull now made the challenge to the old bull. By now the old bull was getting tired. His mouth was frothing and his eyes were red from the physical strain. He had not backed down before, and he wasn't about to back down now. As he pawed the ground he was not as vigorous in his movement as he had been before. Ollikut thought he was surely so exhausted that the young bull would have no trouble making him back down. Yet, he was not sure the old bull would give in.

The two bulls pawed and bellowed for a longer period than before. This gave the old bull a little chance to get his breath. Then came the charge, and the crash! The young bull was knocked to his knees from the momentum. This gave the old bull a chance to back off a step and hit again fast and hard. Being fresh, the young bull quickly regained his footing and met his opponent's next charge, but still he was forced back. The big bull started hooking to the side time and time again. He was not the only one hooking, though. He was taking a beating this time. Blood was now running down his shoulder and out of his chest. A couple more sharp hooks by the old bull and the young bull was down. The old bull bellowed and walked away, but as he did he wobbled and left a trail of blood in three different lines. He would not live out the day. All four of the bulls would die from the combat that Ollikut had watched. What a pity, Ollikut thought, that the old bull had not quit before that last young bull, but he knew he could not have walked away after the first two, either. Admiration filled his chest for the proud old bull that just wouldn't back down.

Now it was time to mount and drop down to the prairie floor where the hunt would begin. Swinging up on Henawit's back, he rode with the others around the bluff and down to the flat. They were now within four hundred yards of the moving herd. Crazy Horse gave the command and all rushed forward for the kill.

Feeling his heart pounding, Ollikut could hardly control the excitement within him. This was much more exciting than any hunting he had ever undertaken before. Never before had he been able to ride to his prey at full speed and be right on top of the game when he shot. Most of his hunting had been with a rifle rather than a bow and arrow. This was the old way and a true test of an Indian's skills at riding and shooting with their ancestor's weapons. All of the hunters were armed this way.

Because of the great number of buffalo, the first animals encountered were not able to get up speed because the ones in front of them were not yet excited. Buffalo began to drop from the Indian's arrows. Then the herd started to run in unison. The Indians had to keep up or be run over. That was when Henawit's speed and endurance became valuable.

Ollikut had had a full quiver of arrows with his mark when they started. The first few he shot were fat young cows and some big yearling calves. These were to be given to the old people when he returned home. With only three arrows left he decided to search out the largest bull he could find. As he glanced around he noticed a huge bull about 100 yards ahead. Urging Henawit on, he raced for the bull. It wasn't long until he was in position for the kill. Drawing back the string, Ollikut let an arrow go to the bull's side. This did not drop the bull. It only made him mad! Tipping his head away from Henawit, the big bull threw a horn into the big horse's shoulder. Henawit jerked with pain as the horn tore the flesh. Ollikut again let an arrow go. He knew he must kill quick or be killed from the stampeding mass of buffalo behind him. This arrow went deep into the body of the bull. A few more steps and down he went.

Ollikut pulled Henawit away to the outside to see how much damage the bull had done. He leaped off and inspected the wound. It was bleeding steadily so Ollikut proceeded to put his hand over the cut to control the blood. Soon Henawit's heart pumping slowed down and the blood coagulated enough that only a little trickle was coming. Ollikut let the big horse stand still, and as his pulse slowed more the bleeding stopped. Once the bleeding stopped, Ollikut took a little water from his water bag and washed the wound off. It did not look as bad once the blood was washed away. Henawit was not limping so Ollikut knew it was only a flesh wound and if cared for, would heal sound.

By now the buffalo herd had rumbled past. As Ollikut looked back, he could see the plains dotted with dead buffalo. He walked to the place he dropped the big bull. As he bent down, the buffalo swung his head in one last effort. The blow hit Ollikut on the calf of his leg, knocking him to the ground. He sprang up with bow in hand and drawing his last arrow, he aimed right at the big bulls heart. Pulling the string back to its full tension, he let the string go. The sharp steel-tip arrow cut through the skin and into the heart of the big beast, ending his movement forever. Ollikut had seen deer react similarly. He should have known better than to get so close to the big bull's head.

Hobbling back to Henawit, Ollikut examined the extent of his own injury. It appeared to be only a bad bruise and luckily nothing was broken. Swinging up on Henawit he slowly rode back towards the bluff where it all began.

By now the families were arriving for the skinning and boning of the dead buffalo. Many of the old bulls would be skinned for their hides, but the meat would be left for the predators because it was too tough to chew. In years gone by nothing would have been left, including the bone, because every piece had a use. Now, with the white man's steel, the bone was no longer needed and only added more weight for the trip home.

The women and dogs all got in on the butchering. It was late evening before all the fat cows and calves had been butchered and the old bulls skinned. The meat and hides were loaded upon the travoises and hauled back to camp.

All Ollikut really wanted was the hide from the powerful old bull. That would help him remember that day for the rest of his life. He and Henawit had made a fine kill with five cows and three yearlings, plus the old bull. That would feed many old people in the Wallowa through the winter.

The meat and hides were too heavy in this condition to pack back across the mountains so the women began slicing the meat in thin strips and letting it dry in the sun. The hides had to be tanned into leather. This process would take many days to complete, even with all the women working at it.

Crazy Horse came to Chief Joseph's camp that night. They talked of the past and the days to come. It was a solemn talk that brought both of them to the realization that the future might be hard. Ollikut passed by where they were sitting.

"That was some fine shooting you did today. I see you got quite a few down. Your arrow mark was plain to see. What I really admired was your mount. That is the finest animal I have ever laid eyes upon," Crazy Horse said.

"Why thank you, Chief. He is my pride. He does just as I ask him. He is a special spirit horse," Ollikut replied.

"I will trade you four of my best horses for him. I need a horse of that great spirit."

"I wouldn't trade him for all your horses. We are tied by our spirit. He was in my dreams before I mated his parents. We shall never part."

"That is a great power you have. He will carry you into many

Henawit

great battles."

"That is what my dream showed me. It has not come to pass. I would rather it did not come, but I am afraid those battles will come."

Ollikut left the two Chiefs to talk. He walked to young Joseph's tepee and sat down next to him.

"Did you have a good hunt?" Ollikut asked.

"Yes, I shot two big yearlings. That will give us more meat than we can use. We will give some to the old."

"Can you see why I would fight for the freedom to come and go as I desire? To come to hunt buffalo as I desire? I can't live under the new treaty."

"We may be forced to live by the new treaty. We may have to move down to the Lapwai reservation. We may have no choice."

"I do not want to live that way."

With that, Ollikut departed for his pack goods and bed roll. He was very tired so sleep came soon. After some time he woke with a start. He had been dreaming that he was in battle with the whites. He was afraid of the outcome but woke before he knew what happened.

With time on their hands waiting for the meat to dry more, Crazy Horse suggested a raid on a Blackfoot camp to obtain horses. This sounded like great sport. Ollikut had always wanted to be on a raiding party, but in the Nez Perce country there were no warring tribes so there were no raids. Everyone was living the slow, peaceful life.

The next morning the warriors left with rations for four days. They had to ride to the Blackfoot country and locate a camp with many horses before being detected. Ollikut did not want to overdo Henawit with his wounded shoulder. He would need him on the long ride back across the mountains. For this ride he picked another big strong horse, but it was not like riding Henawit. He knew what

Henawit would do under stress, but this horse he was not sure of. Young Joseph did not get ready for the raid. He chose to help the elders and women get ready for the trip home.

After a day's ride, they camped by a spring and the raiders got a good rest. The next morning they were up bright and early. By midday they had entered Blackfoot territory. These Indians were the most treacherous of the northwestern Indians. To be captured by them meant certain death.

By dusk the scouts came back with word of a camp about three miles away. There were no guards out. The Blackfoot were so feared they didn't believe anyone would attack them. This was what they had all been waiting for, but it was too close to dark. Crazy Horse said it was better to camp for part of the night then get within striking distance before the first rays of dawn. He was not afraid of the Blackfoot or any other tribe.

It was tough for Ollikut to drop off to sleep that night. All he could think of was the honors of battle if he was strong and fought hard. He thought possibly there would be no battle if the Blackfoot were taken by surprise and left without mounts.

About two hours before dawn, they broke camp and quietly worked their way towards the Blackfoot camp. The Blackfoot had their horse herd split into two parts just in case one herd spooked away they would have the other herd to go after the spooks. The scouts had spotted both herds and Crazy Horse had divided the raiding party into three groups. There would be one group for each herd and one group to attack the main camp.

Ollikut was in the group that was to attack the camp. This he liked for he thought at least he might see battle. They attacked on Crazy Horse's command. All three groups hit at the same time. The Blackfoot did not realize what was happening for a few minutes, but soon they had rifles and bows and were shooting at anything on horseback. The group Ollikut was with galloped full speed through the camp shooting their rifles and whooping and hollering. As soon a warrior was seen, a Sioux or Nez Perce would ride for him and try to count coup by striking him with his club. If they had to kill him to do so, so be it. The raid was not really to kill but to steal from and harass the enemy. It was a game of war rather than a war to the death. The Blackfoot warriors had a different idea of the raid. It was a battle to the death.

After two passes through the camp, Ollikut had counted coup on three Blackfoot warriors just using his war club for a weapon. This would possibly be the last pass through camp for the horse herds were already starting to move towards the north. The Blackfeet were ready this time and Ollikut knew it. He had seen that most had guns by now, and they realized their horses were being stolen. It was like sticking your hand into a hornet's nest to ride through that camp again, but they were south of the camp and had to go north.

This was to be a fast dash through the camp. Ollikut had a lead position for the race. They were off at full speed. Jumping right over one warrior, Ollikut's horse never missed a step. Holding the mane, Ollikut leaned off his horse to hit a warrior a glancing blow before he could aim his rifle. The next thing he knew his horse was shot right out from under him. Down they both went. Tumbling to the side Ollikut escaped being rolled on. A Blackfoot was on top of him before he could gain his feet. There was no time to choose, he must kill or be killed. Pulling his knife, he stuck it to the hilt in the Blackfoot's stomach. Shoving him off, he stood up to see another aiming at him. Instinctively he threw the knife with deadly accuracy, but the gun fired before the knife hit. The sight of the flying knife disturbed the aim of the Blackfoot and the shot missed. Then he saw Yellow Wolf, a cousin, riding hard and sticking his hand down towards him. Ollikut made a hop and a jump grasping Yellow Wolf's hand and vaulted on behind him. Ducking low to the side of the horse they rode out of camp as fast as they could. Bullets were sailing all around them. They saw one Sioux, then another fall from their horses. A Nez Perce then fell. There was nothing that could be done for them; they lay still when they hit the ground.

Yellow Wolf rode next to one of the dead Sioux's horses and Ollikut slipped onto its back. The reins had been tied in a circle over the neck so the rider would not drop them while fighting. With this, Ollikut was all set to ride for camp.

The next day they arrived back at the hunting camp with 53 Blackfoot horses. Ollikut got two good Blackfoot horses, plus he kept the retrieved Sioux's horse. He had lost a good horse and gained three fair horses, but he would have more horses to pack meat on for the long trip home.

They spent another few days in camp playing games, gambling and racing. The women had the meat and robes ready to be packed for the trip over the mountains.

All the way home the people sang and were happy. They had a very successful hunt and a beautiful trip. This was the life they enjoyed and did not want to give up. Why should they stop hunting the buffalo? The white man was hunting them just for the tongue and hides. This was wasteful, but no one stopped them. Ollikut wanted to return to the buffalo country many more times and hunt for this was the true test of a warrior. He had proven himself well and all the young men knew it. They all admired him and would follow his commands. He knew this. It pleased him.

Chapter 10
SOMEONE SPECIAL

Spring came early in 1870. After being in the Wallowa all winter, Ollikut decided to go to Lapwai to buy some goods he needed. It was a beautiful ride down into the basin. As he rode downstream, the grass got greener and more flowers were in bloom. He had never seen the valley so beautiful. This was Ollikut's twenty-fourth summer. He had been so busy breaking horses, trapping and going east to the buffalo that he had thought of little else. These past years, since he left the Spaulding school, had been exciting.

As he rode into Lapwai, he saw Three Moons, who had been baptized Timothy. They called him young Timothy because his father was also called Timothy. Young Timothy was his age. They had been close friends at school. They both talked of the buffalo hunts and fighting the Blackfeet. They both wanted to live the free roaming life, but Timothy's father was satisfied to be a farmer. He was also a very important member of the church, being the second Nez Perce to be baptized. Many times his father would give the sermon in church. It had been Old Timothy and Mr. Spaulding who decided that the punishment for the Nez Perce not doing as the church ordered would be that they were not permitted to attend services on Sunday. This was a punishment the church followers disliked very much. The non-church Nez Perce thought such punishment very silly. They would laugh at the Christians for their strong feelings for the Sunday services.

Ollikut stopped and talked to Young Timothy. Timothy told him of the good harvest they had last year and how he was going to get twenty acres of his own to farm. Timothy showed Ollikut the two work horses he had bought with the money he had made working for others in the community.

"These are fine animals," Ollikut told Timothy. "They appear to be sound and strong. I am sure you will make a good farmer with a fine team such as these."

It was a general practice of the non-treaty Nez Perce to laugh and make fun of those who farmed and went to church. They called them names and even threw sticks at them to see if they would turn the other cheek.

Ollikut took no pleasure in ridiculing the treaty people. He felt sorry for them. He knew many of the young men did not like that way of life but had little chance for anything better.

All the while Ollikut and Timothy had been talking, Timothy hadn't taken his eyes off Henawit. Finally he said, "This is the finest looking horse I have ever seen, Ollikut. He is larger than most, more beautiful and so clean and trim. For a horse like that I would trade all I have, but then I wouldn't know what to do with him because all I know is farming. All of my dreams have died. I only live for today, the planting and the harvest. I shall never know the excitement of the hunt to the east. I have slept well, though, because I have understood these things and accepted them. If I had tasted of the battles and the hunt I could not have accepted my position, but not knowing is better than knowing and desiring something one cannot have."

Just then Timothy's sister, Wetatonmi (Wâ-tÇn'), came out of their father's cabin. Ollikut remembered her from school. She was younger than he and Timothy by a few years. She had changed greatly in the past seven years, Ollikut thought. Then she was a pretty girl and well-liked, but now a beautiful woman.

Wetatonmi was not a large girl. She stood a mere five feet, four inches and was well-formed. Ollikut noticed this at first glance. Her long, silky black hair hung to her waist without any restraints, some of it falling forward over her shoulders. She was trim with no excess of flesh in any place. Her skin sparkled clear and light. Ollikut thought she was beautiful. The sight of her sent tingles all through him. He had been around many girls in the Wallowa, but he had never had this feeling. His father had told him when he found his spirit mate he would instantly know it. Could she be the one?

Wetatonmi

After talking to Timothy and Wetatonmi for a little while, Ollikut told them he had to go to the trading post to get the goods he came for. Timothy, knowing Ollikut had no where to stay in Lapwai, asked if he would come back and have supper and bed down for the night with them. This was more than Ollikut had hoped for, and he happily accepted.

It did not take him long to buy the goods he had come for. He hurried as much as he could. All he could think of was going back to see Wetatonmi.

Timothy was waiting for Ollikut's return, but Wetatonmi was busy helping prepare the cabin for a visitor and arranging for the later meal. On Ollikut's arrival Timothy again admired Henawit. This made Ollikut very pleased, but it also made him sad to think that Timothy would never be able to enjoy Henawit's speed in the race, his agility in battle, or the coordination of horse and man when riding to the buffalo.

"Take him and enjoy the ride. Be very careful how you press your legs, though. Henawit is trained to obey the command of my voice, legs, body and hands. Sometimes it seems he even understands my mind before I give the command with my body. He is my spirit horse," Ollikut said as he handed Timothy the reins.

Henawit was not a horse you could easily step up on. Timothy had to take a big jump to find the stirrup. Then a bounce put him into the saddle. The look of this horse from the saddle was more impressive than from the ground. His neck was full, yet trim. The saddle and skins nearly covered up his short, strong back. This was the finest horse Timothy had ever seen, let alone sat on.

Being accustomed to the slow horses around Lapwai, Timothy kicked Henawit in the ribs rather firmly. Ollikut had never needed a kick, but only a squeeze to get the speed desired. Henawit was not sure what such a kick meant. He dropped his hips, and driving forward, popped Timothy's neck with one jump. In three jumps he was at full speed. Timothy had never traveled so fast and was not too sure he wanted to continue. From fear of falling, he clinched his legs tighter around Henawit's girth. This was the command Ollikut used for more speed so Henawit ran even harder. Timothy realized he must slow down and stop because he was going too fast for his desires. Bracing his feet in the stirrups, Timothy pulled on the reins. Henawit knew a similar command for a fast stop. He sat down on his hind feet and stopped with a five-foot slide. Timothy had not anticipated such a fast stop and found himself with a handful of mane sitting on the neck of Henawit. Patiently the horse stood while Timothy got back in the saddle. Holding a tight rein, Timothy walked back to Ollikut.

"Oh! What a magnificent horse! Did you raise him or did you buy him? I have never seen such a fine horse in all the Nez Perce country." Timothy could hardly stop talking long enough for Ollikut to tell him about Sego Lily and Le Bleu.

At supper Timothy told his father how great a horse Ollikut had raised and how well trained he was. He told how in three jumps he could be flying on the wind, and in the length of a snake he could stop again and be ready to go in any direction commanded.

"This is a true horse for a Nez Perce," said Timothy.

His father slowly pushed his chair away from the table and in a quiet voice answered, "Yes, if you wish to hunt buffalo or go to battle, but he would never do to pull the plow all day or pull the wagon to the mill with a heavy load of grain. For you, my son, the slow but powerful horse will do."

Timothy's eyes dropped and his face grew thin. Yes, he knew he would not, in this life, need such a horse as this. But, oh, if only he did.

Old Timothy was not too pleased with Ollikut staying the night. Ollikut was a non-Christian Indian and was considered a heathen because of his dress and way of living, as well as his attitude towards the church. He had been given a white man's name but never used it. He never showed enough interest in the church for the Spauldings to pursue his religious education.

Ollikut's presence that night had roused desires in Young Timothy that the elder Timothy had tried to bury over the years. Young Timothy had almost given up any ideas of the other life. Wetatonmi, however, was not as easy to dissuade. Because of this, she had not yet been baptized. She still wanted to wear buckskin dresses split up the middle so she might ride like a man. The rest of the young ladies in Lapwai had bought cloth from the trading post and made dresses and aprons as well as all of the undergarments that Mrs. Spaulding had shown them how to make. They were as close to being white as any Indian could be.

Not Wetatonmi. She was Nez Perce and proud of it. She loved the wild country and had a pony that she rode almost every day. To be among the hills in the spring was essential to her very existence. To see the flowers in bloom, the deer bounding through the woods and to watch the beaver rebuild their homes for the summer were the things that gave her life meaning. Old Timothy knew this. He tried to discourage the rides. He would give her tasks in the house, even in the field, to occupy her time because the Bible told him that idle hands do the devils's work.

All through supper Ollikut could hardly take his eyes off Wetatonmi. He knew he had never felt like this before. When their eyes met, he could tell she wanted to see into his mind, as he did hers. After supper he watched her as she helped around the cabin, cleaning up the table and making beds for the night. He could see she was capable in the cabin. He thought . . . How would she be in a tepee?

His father had once told him to pick a wife the way you pick a horse. She must be strong of build with full shoulders for carrying water and strong legs for walking beside the pack horses when moving camp. She should be of calm temper with enough thought of mind for a woman's tasks, but not so much as to advise a man on the tasks he was to do. She should have well-rounded hips for childbearing and be well V'd up in the chest to provide enough milk for the baby.

But Wetatonmi did not look like a work horse. She looked like a running horse. She was drawn up in the belly with no excess rump. Her legs were trim and clean like the legs of a deer. Her actions were quick and her temper evident. She had a mind of her own as could be seen by her dress and actions.

Was this not the type of woman he should seek? Should he wait until he found one that matched his father's description of a good wife?

Ollikut was not used to sleeping on a bed with a woven rope bottom. Being just under six feet tall, he hung over the bed on each end and sank very low in the middle. Getting to sleep seemed impossible. Finally, he gave up the bed and pulled the blankets to the floor with him. This did not bring him sleep either. It wasn't the bed; it was inside his head. All he could think of was the beautiful Wetatonmi. After laying awake thinking for sometime, he finally fell asleep, tossing, turning and dreaming the rest of the night. His dreams included Wetatonmi, Henawit and himself. Was his dream to be true, he wondered.

The next morning breakfast was set and the men ate first. This was a working day and Timothy and his father had more crops to plant. Keeping the weeds out of the crops already up was a never-ending job in the spring.

Ollikut intended to leave early that morning, but for some reason did not get his horse saddled and packed until after the breakfast dishes were done and Wetatonmi had come out of the house. Wetatonmi had also admired Ollikut's fine horse. She loved horses and riding. She came close to Henawit. He seemed to realize she admired him; he put his nose out and touched her on the cheek. Wiggling his nose, he tickled her face. It was love at first sight. Ollikut could see the two had made friends. He told Wetatonmi she could ride if she would be very careful and go slow. He didn't want the same thing to happen to her that had happened to Timothy.

After a leg up, Wetatonmi settled into the saddle. She was not accustomed to using a saddle for her father did not have one and would not buy one for her. Not being able to reach the long stirrups, she sat as if riding bareback. Leaning slightly forward while squeezing her legs, she moved Henawit off in a slow gallop. She rode with style and grace. Ollikut could tell that Henawit was responding to every command with ease. When rider and horse were coordinated as Wetatonmi and Henawit, the action was as one.

She ran Henawit back to Ollikut and stopped dead still in front of him.

"This is a horse of the wind," Wetatonmi said as she jumped down. "If only my horse could fly like yours!"

Earlier that morning Ollikut had observed the old pony she was speaking of. He knew she could not go fast or far on that horse.

Knowing it might be sometime before he came down to the basin again, and knowing he wanted to spend as much time as possible with her, he asked her to ride up to the hills with him. Any other Christian girl in Lapwai would have said no. Indeed, a Christian woman wouldn't have been allowed to talk to a heathen at all. Wetatonmi grabbed her bridle and was mounted before Ollikut could finish tying on his goods behind the saddle.

It was a beautiful ride. The birds were singing and the sweet aroma of the flowers in bloom stung them both with a new kind of fire. Every time their eyes met, their gaze went much deeper than the face. It penetrated into the mind. Ollikut knew, to his satisfaction, that she wanted to see him again.

As they reached the hills, Ollikut stopped and asked her if she should return now. One look into his eyes and she knew that was not what he wanted.

Jumping off, she held out her hand and said, "Let us walk together for a while, then I will return."

Grasping her hand, Ollikut felt emotions he had never before experienced. He felt warm inside with a calm contentment, yet a burning desire all at the same time. He wondered if such feelings were wrong or should he enjoy them. Feeling the warmth of her hand, he knew this couldn't be wrong. It was easy for him to talk to her, and she soon knew of his feelings for his horse as well as for her. She respected him for the way he treated his horse and the way he'd worked to develop the bond that was between them. She felt sure he would treat her with kindness and develop a bond with her, too.

After walking and talking for more than an hour, Ollikut finally stopped. "You must go back now. Your father will worry and your mother will need your help."

Ollikut told her to give him her leg and he would help her on. Both of them knew very well she could mount her pony with one jump. She lifted her foot for Ollikut to help her on. In one smooth motion she was astride her pony. She had never had a man offer to help her mount before that day. Such a courtesy. She had only heard of the white men giving their ladies assistance.

Ollikut mounted Henawit and rode to the side of Wetatonmi. Grasping her hand and looking deep into her eyes, Ollikut said, "I will be back before the next moon with a gift."

All the way home Ollikut thought of what he might bring her that would make her heart most full of joy. He thought of the beautiful moccasins his mother had made or the necklaces that had been made from shells collected at the great waters to the west.

Arriving back home he still had not decided what gift would be best. He knew he had not remembered a thing of the ride home. All he could remember were the thoughts of Wetatonmi. It was good that Henawit knew the way home or the pair might have been lost for days.

Instead of tethering Henawit close to his tepee, Ollikut decided to take him to the meadow where he could graze with the rest of his horses. As he approached his small band, he saw the two-year-old son of Henawit he was so proud of. Ollikut had not named this horse yet and still called him "the colt." This fine son of Henawit was a good-sized bay with four white legs and a blaze down his forehead. He was marked like Henawit with a full white blanket and dark spots. Now there, he thought, is the horse for a Nez Perce princess to ride.

The next day Ollikut caught the colt and gelded him so that he would be more docile than if left a stallion. This made the colt forget about the opposite sex and just worry about himself. Ollikut rode out each day and drove all the horses around the meadow. This exercise kept the colt's incision open and permitted drainage and healing from within. Within two weeks the colt was as good as new and ready for the journey to Lapwai.

A few days later Ollikut arrived at Lapwai with the colt. The trip had been a new experience for the colt, and he had learned to lead better and respect the rope when it was tightened.

Chapter 11

THE GIFT

It was almost dusk by the time Ollikut reached Old Timothy's cabin. He tied the horses in the corral and went to the door of the cabin. Wetatonmi had not heard or seen his approach. When she saw him at the door she was so surprised she could not hold back the pleased look in her eyes. Yet, the greeting was just cordial. Her mother barely said hello to Ollikut. Her father and brother were not yet home from the mission mill.

Ollikut asked her to come see what he had brought as her gift. As darkness was setting in and no one would see, Ollikut took her hand in his as they ran to the corral. The colt stood tied to a post near the gate. Wetatonmi did not realize that the colt was her present, but she thought that the colt was beautiful, almost as beautiful as the great Henawit himself.

"This is the best present I have to offer. This colt is the son of Henawit. He is built with strength and beauty. I want him to be your partner," Ollikut said.

The colt was standing with his neck bowed and his nostrils wide. His eyes were ablaze with wonder for he had not seen a woman before or smelled the sweet smell that came from Wetatonmi's hair. With one look, Wetatonmi could see the colt was all horse and a little on the wild side.

"I did not have time to train him after I gelded him. He will be a handful to handle. You will have to go slow. Maybe Timothy can help you some. I will come down and help you

111

once you bond with him," Ollikut told Wetatonmi.

Wetatonmi could not speak for loss of words. She wanted so to have a fine horse, but she had never even let herself dream of such a horse as this. "You should not give such a gift, Ollikut. This could have made you a buffalo horse or even a war horse. He is finer than most chiefs ride. No woman has ever had a finer animal. I will care for him like a mother for her child and love him until he trusts me and loves me. I will call him Partner. He will be my partner, I'm sure."

The next morning Old Timothy saw the horse and was very displeased. He had been trying for years to get Wetatonmi to forget about horses. He wanted her to take up the domestic life of a white woman. Now he would have even more trouble. This also could affect Young Timothy. Only heathens needed fast, colorful war horses, not a maiden or a young farmer. He told Ollikut of his thoughts, but Ollikut said a gift was given and could not be taken back.

"Ollikut, I don't want this horse in my corral. The elders will think I have taken up the heathen ways. I don't want my children taking up the heathen ways either. You have brought bad medicine into my home. The horse must go."

"A gift is a gift. Only a white man or a bad Indian would take a gift back after he gave it. I'm not a bad Indian trader. This gift is of much value and you should take good care to feed him well."

Because of the bad feelings shown him by Old Timothy, Ollikut decided to leave for home early the next morning. Again, Wetatonmi rode out to the hills with him. On the way he advised her how to handle her new partner and at all times to be careful because he didn't want her to get hurt.

As they approached the hills, they dismounted and walked up the draw to a nice grassy opening where the horses could graze and they could sit and talk.

Taking Wetatonmi's hand, Ollikut said, "My thoughts are filled with visions of you day and night. I can smell the scent of your hair in the dust of every flower. The memory of the touch of your soft, warm hands lingers with me always."

She, too, had thought of nothing else for the past two weeks. "You are the man I have been waiting to meet. Many Lapwai men have desired to marry me, but I did not want to be a farmer's wife and live at Lapwai the rest of my life. I wanted more. I wanted to see the plains to the east, to live in the mountains where the wild things still are free, to ride with my husband and help him raise fine spotted horses. These things are in my heart. I know I could never be happy on a farm when all that horse country is here, and now you Ollikut."

After sitting and talking for hours, they knew they must part; nevertheless they could hardly tear away from one another. A fire was burning in them both, a fire that couldn't be quenched. They knew their love would have its day. With a kiss and a fond caress, Ollikut assisted her onto her pony. "I will return with another gift for you before the passing of another moon."

For the next two weeks Wetatonmi spent every minute she could with Partner. She made friends with him and he started to trust her. The progress she was making made her very happy.

Timothy admired the gift almost as much as his sister. He wanted to help her with the training of the colt. One day while Wetatonmi was exercising Partner on the rope, Timothy offered to help. Working with the colt was not going too well. Timothy walked towards his rear end to spook him, but the colt didn't spook. Up came his rear end and out went a hoof. It caught Timothy right on the temple, knocking him to the ground. Timothy did not move. Wetatonmi thought maybe he was dead. She called for her father and they took him in the house. Timothy was still breathing so they put cold packs on his head. After about an hour, Timothy started coming to. The rest of the day he lay in bed with a very bad headache.

"The colt must go before you or Timothy get killed," Old Timothy said.

"It was not Partner's fault, it was my own for getting so close to the colt's rear. The colt did not know me and kicked out of fear. That is something Partner does not have for Wetatonmi," Young Timothy said.

Feeling very sorry for Timothy, Wetatonmi went to the corral and scolded Partner for what he had done, but she knew he was not a mean colt. He had run loose for two years and was finding it hard to forget his wild ways.

Partner

114

Partner's training, from then on, was undertaken with more care and understanding of his power. Wetatonmi would tell everyone to stay back because the colt was not gentle and might kick them. She also was more on guard while working around him. The training went very well and at the end of two weeks she thought it was time to start teaching him about the saddle and blanket. Borrowing an old Indian saddle from a neighbor, she began his training. She let Partner smell the blanket and the saddle, then she tossed the blanket on and off a number of times until he was no longer afraid of it. Then came the saddle. This wasn't quite as easy. He jumped sideways the first try. It took sometime before she could get them both on at once. Tightening the belly strap also took time. The colt did not like the feel of the strap underneath his belly. He finally relaxed, mostly because he trusted her and wanted to please her.

Next came the bridle. The Nez Perce farmers had adopted the white man's bit so this was what she had to use. It was a bit with round circles on the sides and a broken bar for a mouth piece like that used by Timothy's work horses. By sliding her thumb into the side of Partner's mouth and pressing down, she was able to get him to open his mouth. She turned Partner loose in the corral with the saddle and bridle on. He walked around the corral, chewing on the bit while trying to spit it out. It just wouldn't come out. The colt was turned loose with the saddle and bridle for a little while each day until he got used to them.

She had worked with him long enough. The first ride had to come. She decided this would be the day. Partner had been saddled for sometime just walking and trotting around the corral with his head tied one way and then the other. Pulling his head towards her with the rein, Wetatonmi put a foot into the stirrup and stepped on. The colt didn't know what to do with the weight. She didn't give him time to find out. She turned him into the fence one way and then the other for about ten minutes. Then she dismounted. That was enough for the first ride, she thought.

She rode Partner in the corral for a few times, then they went out the gate towards the hills. Wetatonmi had not ridden many different horses before, but she knew from those she had ridden that this colt had a fine walk. He was very sure-footed from running in the Wallowa all his life. His trot was smooth and easy. Ollikut had told her not to gallop or run the colt until he was handling well so she only let him trot. He soon learned to carry her weight. He moved with grace and agility.

Wetatonmi could not believe that this was her horse and that she had started to break him by herself. This was what she had always dreamed of but never thought it could come true. She knew she was not like the other girls in Lapwai, but this did not concern her. All her hopes and her thoughts were now with Ollikut and Partner.

Chapter 12

A CHANGE OF LIFE

The past month had gone by quickly for Ollikut. He had been breaking horses for members of the tribe. He would break three horses with the understanding that he could keep one. The owner could choose the two he wanted when the three were broke. This was one way Ollikut could build up his herd. The mares not good enough to use for breeding and the poorer geldings could be sold to the whites or to the occasional Indian trading party that crossed the mountains in search of the spotted horse of many colors. There was no problem selling or trading unwanted horses. There were always more who wanted horses than there were horses for sale.

A band of friendly Sioux came into camp just after Ollikut had finished riding for the day. They had come to buy horses. They brought trading goods and some gold. The next day they rode through the herds of horses and marveled at their beauty. The head Sioux warrior spotted Henawit and said, "This is the horse I wish." He was told Henawit belonged to Ollikut. Upon their return to camp, the Sioux went to talk to Ollikut.

"I wish to buy your war horse Henawit."

"I am happy you chose my great spirit horse but he would not like living with anyone else. We have been to your buffalo hunts and shot many buffalo. He can do all the things you would like but he only works from my movements."

"What would you sell me? The poor non-colored horses?"

"I have a fine mare bred to my great one. She has a likeness of Henawit inside her. I was going to keep her, but I will trade her for gold and the saddle you ride. This is the only way you will get the likeness of Henawit. You can see from his other colts that he does produce his likeness."

The Sioux finally decided he would not get Henawit and agreed to the trade. The Sioux left the next morning with forty head of ponies, most of which were less quality than the average spotted horse, but they were still superior to the small plains ponies they were accustomed to riding.

Late that evening he heard Henawit whinnying with an excited tone. Ollikut looked out his tepee opening just in time to see the Sioux horse trader mounting Henawit.

Stepping out of the tepee, Ollikut gave a shrill whistle. Henawit spun around and ran right for Ollikut. There was nothing the Sioux could do to stop him.

"I was just trying your horse to see how great he is."

"I told you he only responds to my commands. He knows how I think and I know how he thinks. We work through the spirit."

"I will run and catch my friends."

"I think we will have a chance to count coup right now. Get off my horse and we will see how a horse thief fights."

"I don't want to fight you. You are just a young warrior. It wouldn't be fair."

"Let me decide what is fair. I know stealing my horse isn't fair. Should it be knives or lances that settles this?"

"If we must fight, I will chose lances."

Ollikut picked up a couple of lances that were standing next to his tepee. Tossing one to the horse thief, he positioned himself so the thief couldn't get to the trail out of camp.

The thief jabbed at Ollikut a number of times. The next jab, Ollikut swung and knocked the lance out of his opponents hands.

"Pick up your lance, thief. I want you to say I was fair before I kill you."

"But if you kill me, how can I tell everyone how fair you are?"

"That's true. Maybe I will just hurt you bad."

They jousted some more until the thief moved quickly to strike Ollikut. As he charged in, Ollikut stepped to the side and drove the lance into the ground between the thief's legs causing him to go down in a heap.

As he rose with his rear end up first, Ollikut struck him across the rump as hard as he could. The thief sprawled out on the ground. Ollikut stepped over the Sioux setting the point of his lance over the Indian's heart.

"Now you go back to your Sioux tribe and tell Chief Crazy Horse that you met Ollikut of the Wallowa Nez Perce. Tell him of the bad deeds you tried. I'm sure he will be displeased that you would try to steal his friend's great horse."

"I will tell him. Thank you for sparing my life. I will try to be a better horse thief next time." With that, the Sioux jumped up and started running up the trail to catch his friends.

Ollikut was pleased with what he had done. He remembered killing before. It didn't make him feel good. He would only kill if there was no alternative.

The saddle the Sioux rode was one of the finest saddles Ollikut had seen. It was the finest of Sioux workmanship. Ollikut picked a prime fur pelt to cover the saddle and set them with a new bridle he had made. The next morning he caught Henawit and a pack horse and down to Lapwai he went. This time he rode like the wind. He could hardly wait to show Wetatonmi the gift he had for her. Most of all, he could not wait any longer to see her. She had been in his dreams day and night. While breaking horses he had thought how nice it would be to have her riding with him as he rode the colts through the hills. By now he knew he must have her for his wife.

It was midday by the time Ollikut reached Lapwai. He rode straight for Old Timothy's cabin. Wetatonmi was in the corral talking to Partner and brushing him. His hair was short and glistened like sun upon water. She had ridden him and then groomed him until his beautiful color was at its utmost brilliance. Ollikut could see the love that existed between these two. He could see the care and work that had been given to produce such a fine finish on the colt. Ollikut was pleased

Stepping down from Henawit, Ollikut tied his horses to the corral. Wetatonmi left Partner and ran to where he was. Even though it was daylight and others might see, he took her hand in his. This time neither of them cared. Looking up at him she said, "My heart is filled with joy when I see you here as the brook fills with water when the snow melts in the spring. I feel glad as the ponies do when the fresh grass starts in the beginning of its growth."

"You have that colt looking like a piece of the sun. He sparkles from nose to tail."

"Just wait until you see how well he responds to the cues you told me about."

"To ride such a fine horse one must have a fine saddle and bridle. Here is yours," he said as he uncovered the new saddle and bridle he had tied onto the pack horse.

"This is more than my heart could desire," she told him. "Now I have the finest saddle, as well as the finest horse in Lapwai. This is more than I should take from you. It is too much."

Ollikut thought for a moment and asked, "Is it not proper for a warrior to give his wife gifts?"

"Yes, but I am not your wife," said Wetatonmi.

"Well, we must change that as soon as possible if this is your wish also."

"That is my wish and has been for sometime, Ollikut," she said.

Packing her few belongings, she was ready to go within the hour. Her mother, Tamar, begged her not to go to the heathen life but to stay at Lapwai and find a Christian that would give her a cabin and a stable life.

"Mother, some people are born to be free while others are content to be secure within a cabin with an agent to protect them. Wetatonmi is not like us. She is like the wind that blows in the night and the water that runs in the stream. She must go where she will and Ollikut will protect her with his mind and his strength. Ollikut has many horses and can give her things that a farmer could never buy. She should have a life of her choosing, not just an existence on a reservation," said Young Timothy.

Weeping, her mother caressed Wetatonmi, then turned and entered another room.

Timothy told her, "I will tell father of your wishes. I know he will not understand, but this is your life and you must choose the way it is to be so go with a smile and don't look back. In time the hurt will leave this house and then you should return to make peace and comfort our parents."

Once the packhorse was loaded and Partner saddled and bridled, Ollikut helped Wetatonmi up, then mounted Henawit. Waving good-by to Timothy, they rode for the Wallowa.

Upon arriving at Wallowa, Ollikut told his father of his plans. His father was very pleased and agreed to marry them soon. The women needed time to prepare Wetatonmi for the marriage and help her build a tepee.

Building a tepee did not come naturally to Wetatonmi. She had lived all her life at Lapwai in a cabin and had seen few tepees. Because her father farmed, there was little time to visit other places. The church also taught them to stay at home and be satisfied with what they had. Because of this, she had little exposure to the rest of the world and knew little of different ways of living such as those of the Wallowa band.

The women of the camp all helped her cut poles for the tepee and sew the buffalo hides together properly. They showed her how to stretch them over the poles. As a wife she was expected to know how to make and break camp. In case of a battle the men would hold off the attackers and the women and children, with the help of the older people, had to break camp and start to move to a new site. The women showed her that the top must be open and that the front entrance flap should face toward the breeze. If not, the smoke from the cooking fire would all stay inside the tepee and the tepee would be of no use. She didn't realize how important this would be.

Ollikut's mother made Wetatonmi a beautiful white buckskin dress for her wedding day. It was decorated with red beads and fringed at the arms and around the bottom. This was the finest dress Wetatonmi had ever had for she was accustomed to buying hides at the trading post. She could not afford the better skins and sometimes bought material of the white man's making because it was easier to sew than the hides. Ollikut's mother also gave her a pair of moccasins covered with red beads, a belt trimmed in red and a fine bag in which she could carry her possessions.

After building the tepee and having been told of the things that a husband would expect of his wife, she was prepared for the ceremony. The wedding was set for the next morning. Wetatonmi slept very little that night despite being tired from all the preparation.

Ollikut was not doing much better. They had only seen glimpses of each other since he had told his father of his plans a few weeks before. He so wanted to be with her. It had been much too long since first he knew that he must have her for his wife.

The morning brought the promise of a beautiful day, full of sunshine and clear skies. The birds were singing and squirrels scampered up and down the trees chattering back and forth. Ollikut had risen early and gone to the river for a cold bath. All he could think of was how happy he was and how happy Wetatonmi would make him. After the bath, he then covered his body with a light coating of oil which made his skin shine. He put on his finest buckskins. He wore his hair straight from the sides, with the center pushed forward to form a rise. Holding his hair in place was a beaded head band.

Wetatonmi had risen early, too. After her dip in the river, she too put on a sweet smelling oil that made her skin glisten in the morning light. Her long black hair was combed into two flocks, one falling down the front of each shoulder. Close to her head nestled in her hair were round beaded ornaments with rawhide tie strings. These were tied in place to hold her hair. No heart held more joy than hers, she thought, as she pulled on her red moccasins and dressed in the clothes Ollikut's mother had made for her.

It was now time for the women to come get Wetatonmi and take her to the council circle where the marriage would take place. She was pleased that the women had accepted her and treated her so kindly. These were good people, the kind she wanted to spend her life with.

Looking taller and more proud than ever, Ollikut stood in the circle waiting for his bride.

Ollikut could hardly believe his eyes when Wetatonmi finally appeared. Her hair shone in the morning sun like light itself. She looked trim and beautiful in the white buckskin dress. The red in the outfit made it bright and happy. Wetatonmi was smiling deep from within. Her eyes sparkled with happiness.

Here were two people very much in love and happy with the thought of being joined as one. Their hearts had been intertwined for the past few months. Now their lives would be set on the same trail.

Old Chief Joseph entered the circle when the marriage group had formed. Holding his hands up arms length above his head he said, "My people, this day is a very special day for my son, Ollikut, and his bride to be. It is also a very happy day for me. Ollikut is my brave warrior son and the light of my eye. He has pleased me with his deeds as he has grown up. He pleases me now in the choice he has made for a wife. Wetatonmi may not be the size of a wife I would pick, but because of her heart she is a better choice."

"Ollikut, the Great Spirit is pleased with you too, I'm sure. He will show his pleasure by giving you a fine son as he gave you to me. His guidance will be with you and protect you so that you may enjoy your wife and your son. Always be proud of your family and your own deeds and the Great Spirit will be proud, too."

"Now I bind your hands together as your hearts and bodies will be bound together in marriage. From this time forward you will be known as husband and wife. Always protect your wife and treat her well, Ollikut. And you, Wetatonmi, always watch after Ollikut's needs and make him proud he is your husband. Be with him day or night when he needs you and accept that he will need to be away at times. Always be true to his honor while he is away and greet him with joy upon his return."

Ollikut

124

"You are married now as one. Before the next sunrise be gone for your time alone," Joseph said.

Ollikut took Wetatonmi into his arms and raised her off the ground squeezing her very tightly for a long moment. Joy filled them both!

After the feast Ollikut and Wetatonmi lay on the soft, sweet-smelling grass and watched the activities. Most of the time, however, was spent looking at each other.

Even though Ollikut was entranced with the idea of being a married man, he could not forget about the excitement of the games. Finally, Wetatonmi said, "My husband, I have not seen you test Henawit and it would please me to see that."

This pleased Ollikut. He was proud of his horse and the ability they both exhibited when they were together.

Running to where Henawit was tied, he untied him, threw the reins over his neck and up he went onto Henawit's back. Henawit had heard the whooping and hollering that was going on and knew it meant games and races. He was alive with eagerness as he loped to where the games were taking place. The stump race and stake race were already over but the buffalo hunt race was about to begin. This race was practiced for the actual buffalo hunts to the east. A yearling steer was held at a distance of one hundred feet from the rider. The rider was equipped with a lance and a piece of hide tied around its' tip end. The hide was dipped in a jar of white dye.

At the rider's signal the steer was released to run the quarter mile back to the cow herd. The rider was to catch up to the steer and strike it with the lance in a vital spot as soon as he could. With the steer having a head start, this took a fast horse.

Eleven riders had already tried. Three had touched the steer with the lance, but only one had touched a vital point. This was at the last moment before the steer entered the herd.

It was Ollikut's turn next. Henawit knew what would be expected of him from previous games. His eyes were on the steer. When Ollikut signaled to turn the steer loose, the strong horse dropped his haunches and dug in for the chase. Within three jumps he was at full speed. He covered the first one hundred feet in a streak. By the time he had gone two hundred yards he was on the hip of the steer. Ollikut leaned over and touched the steer right behind the front shoulder about a foot from the top of the steer's back. From this angle a true lance would penetrate down into the heart and lungs if this had been a chase for the kill. Ollikut had made his coup with still many yards left to run had he needed them.

After watching the previous eleven riders, Wetatonmi was very impressed with Ollikut and Henawit's performance. This made Ollikut very happy.

Next came the races. The race consisted of two parts. The first was a hundred yard run to reach a lance, retrieve it, get back to the starting line, throw the lance at a target, then turn and race two miles over all kinds of terrain, finishing at the starting line. This required a horse with quick speed, fast turns and stops, and plenty of endurance. The Nez Perce always gave their mounts extreme tests to see which ones would have the heart to go after their body said stop.

There were five horses in the race. Ollikut knew that these were the very fastest in the Wallowa. Anyone who did not have a very fast horse did not even attempt to run against Henawit. As they broke from the starting line, Henawit took the lead. Reaching the lance, he pivoted around it as Ollikut picked it up. They were ahead by a full length. As they made the turn and started back towards the starting line, a slow horse still going the other way collided with him on an angle. This, with his own speed, threw Henawit to the side. He tried to catch his balance but could not, falling with his shoulder to the ground.

Ollikut stepped off as Henawit went down. He had no more gone down than he was scrambling up again. As he rose, Ollikut slid a leg over his back and was on and ready when Henawit again gained his legs. They were soon off and running but over six lengths behind the others.

Wetatonmi's heart jumped when she saw the fall. She could not see through the dust of the riders coming towards the starting line so she could not see that Ollikut was safe. All she could think of was that Ollikut had been rolled on. She had seen other riders that were rolled on and knew the damage that could happen. Rising, she was about to run to Ollikut when she finally saw him. This was a big relief. She surely did not want to lose her husband on their wedding day.

Throwing the lance to the center of the target at the starting line, Ollikut turned Henawit and took out after the others. The other horses were all good long distance runners. They did not have the fast burst of speed that Henawit had, but that would do him no good now. Could Henawit slowly but surely catch and pass the other four horses? He did not have time to pace himself over the distance. If he were to win, he would have to run hard and fast.

After a mile he was just about to catch the last rider. Slowly but surely he pulled on by him. This was good, but the leader was still six lengths ahead. Ollikut knew that Henawit felt the pain in his shoulder and the burning in his lungs from the fast pace he had to run to catch up. With a half mile left to go, there were still two horses ahead of him.

Ollikut realized the strain placed on Henawit. He did not want to win badly enough to hurt his horse so he let Henawit decide how fast he would take the last half mile.

There was just too much burning desire in Henawit to be first. With a final effort he drove off every muscle and pulled the same way as he covered the ground. He was running on pure heart now! His leg and shoulder hurt. The burning in his lungs and throat was painful. On he ran, passing the next horse in slow motion. There was only one horse in front of him and just one hundred yards left to run and run he did! Ollikut thought his horse was running the first one hundred yards the way he flew to the finish line just ahead of the other horse.

Henawit was about exhausted and Ollikut knew it. He jumped off and patted the horse with much approval. They both knew that they had given their all. Wetatonmi ran up and told Ollikut she wanted to walk Henawit while he cooled down for the sweat was running off his belly from the long, hard run. This pleased Ollikut to think his wife would desire to walk Henawit and take pride in him as she did Ollikut.

Ollikut took Henawit down to the creek after he was cooled off and let him stand in water up to his shoulders. After a cool bath all over, Ollikut packed mud on his leg and shoulder where the pain was. This drew out the soreness and made Henawit feel much better.

Ollikut expected much out of his horses, but he always took good care to see they were fed and comfortable and doctored when necessary.

The next morning Henawit was feeling much better and ready for an easy ride to the place Ollikut had chosen to take his bride. Wetatonmi rode Partner and they led two pack horses with a two-week's supply of goods.

These two weeks were beautiful. They camped in a shady draw near a spring. Each day they rode, talked and dreamed. Ollikut killed fresh game for them as they needed it. This was the most peaceful time he had had in his life. He was not used to this much peace and soon became restless, but Wetatonmi took care of that.

At the end of the two weeks they packed their goods. Taking a last long look at their comfortable retreat, they headed for the main camp and their new life.

Chapter 13
TRAPPING TROUBLE

The remainder of the summer Ollikut broke horses. His new wife, not having much work at camp, rode with him almost every day. Ollikut enjoyed her companionship, also her help with the breaking. She had learned much while breaking Partner. Ollikut put her new knowledge to good use. Once he got the horses started and had them so they did not wish to buck, he let Wetatonmi train them to obey leg, body, hand and voice commands.

Being a gentle person, she brought gentleness to her training. The horses responded more quickly to her training than they had generally done to his more aggressive methods. Ollikut was very pleased with his wife and the help she gave him. This was a beautiful life in a wonderful land.

As fall set in, the fur-bearing animals began growing their winter coats. It was time to start setting traps and collecting pelts. This was man's work but Wetatonmi often rode with him to check the traps.

Trapping was good and Ollikut soon had many hides with all winter ahead in which to get more. With these hides he would buy guns and ammunition as well as knives and other white man's goods that would help him to hunt and trap more game. He would also buy goods for Wetatonmi so she would have an easier time making a good home for them.

While emptying the traps, Ollikut noticed the tracks of a big, brown bear. He could see that she had two cubs with her. This was a bear to stay away from, Ollikut thought to himself. A mother bear with cubs to protect was one of the most vicious creatures a man could meet in the Wallowa.

Walking downstream Ollikut came across the boot tracks of a white man. Next he came to his empty trap that had held a beaver. Someone had taken the beaver. He had stolen from him what was rightfully his. Ollikut followed the boot tracks until he came to a makeshift cabin. He could see the white man outside the cabin. Ollikut approached the white man to see if he could prove it was he who had stolen the beaver. No white man had a right to be trapping in the Wallowa. This was agreed to in the 1855 treaty. This man had no right building a cabin, let alone stealing beaver.

Ollikut saw, as he approached the cabin, that there were two, freshly-skinned beaver pelts stretched and drying in the warm sun. What should he do? Should he kill this man? He was angry enough, but that was not his father's way and killing would just cause more killing.

The trapper finally saw Ollikut and, not knowing it was Ollikut's traps he had robbed, signaled for him to come closer. Ollikut approached the trapper apprehensively for he did not want to be killed either. The trapper was a large, robust man with a beard. He was in his mid to late thirties and by all looks a strong man.

The trapper asked, "Have you seen any bear? That's what I'm looking for."

"There have been fewer bears this year than usual because of the long, hard winter last year. Some of the bears died before they could find enough to eat in the spring," Ollikut told him.

Just then Ollikut thought of a way to get even with this trapper and possibly run him out of the Wallowa without killing him. Remembering seeing the tracks of the mother bear and her cubs, he thought, here is a bear for this trapper.

"I saw some tracks this morning. I will go and locate the bear and come back and tell you where to find it. Wait inside your cabin until I come back."

Jogging back upstream, Ollikut soon came to the tracks of the bear. He determined which way she was headed and took off tracking her as fast as he could. He hadn't gone more than half a mile from the cabin when he heard the cubs playing and fighting. Soon he saw them in a small clearing rolling around and growling at each other. He could not see the she bear anywhere but knew she must be close by. He knew if he was not careful he could be killed by her, too. Sneaking in as close as he could to the brush, he watched them play for a few moments. They had not sensed his presence so far and were moving in his direction. One gave the other a big shove and he went rolling, landing within an arm's reach of Ollikut. Reaching down, he grabbed the cub by the back of the neck. This brought a loud cry from the cub. He thought that would surely bring the mother bear but nothing happened so he reached down and twisted the cub's ear. This brought all kinds of wailing and shrieking from the cub. In a flash the mother bear broke through into the clearing. She had come from upstream as Ollikut had thought she might.

With the cub in his arms, Ollikut jumped up and started running. The cub was screaming and clawing. The mother bear wasted no time in making tracks toward Ollikut. By now the cub was more than he could handle so he dropped him and ran as fast as he could. The mother bear ran to the cub, paused to check it, then seeing the cub was okay, took out after Ollikut. Ollikut was a very fast runner but he had over half a mile to go and that bear wasn't slow. Having a head start helped, but not for long because the bear could run longer and faster than Ollikut. All he could hope was that he could reach the cabin.

They covered the first quarter mile in record time, but Ollikut could see the bear was gaining on him. He knew he could not run any faster. All he could hope was that the bear was getting winded, too. With the cabin now in sight Ollikut could almost feel the breathing of the bear behind him but did not dare turn to see. He knew she was within ten feet of him and still gaining. If only he could outrun her to the door, he thought. With one more driving effort, he made it to the door with the bear less than two feet behind him. The door was open and Ollikut burst in. As he did he saw the trapper lying on the bedroll. All he could see was the trapper jump up as the bear came through the door. Ollikut grabbed the door and stepped back out, then closed the latch.

Now the trapper had more bear than he had planned on. The bear mauled him around some before he could break free. Ollikut knew the trapper must get out, and fast! He could see through a hole in the roof the trapper was swinging the barrel of his rifle to hold her off long enough to move to the hole left for a window in the side of the cabin. With one great effort he hit the bear, then turned and flew through the hole. The bear grabbed for his legs, tearing his pants and ripping into the flesh.

Grabbing a mauled and broken arm the trapper hobbled to his makeshift corral, caught his horse and rode off for the low country as fast as he could. Ollikut ran to the cover of the timber around the cabin and waited to see what the bear would do. After the trapper rode off he could still hear that bear tearing things up in the cabin. Ollikut decided after all the help the bear had been he should not leave her locked up so he broke a long branch off a nearby tree and climbed back up on the roof of the cabin. By lying on his stomach he was able, with the aid of the stick, to release the latch and push open the door. Once the bear saw the open door she ran out. Standing on her hind legs, sniffing and looking all around, she hesitated. She was still on the prod and finding a foe would fight to the death. Ollikut stayed down so he couldn't be seen. He was downwind from her but still quite close. He thought for a moment she had caught his scent, but then she turned and loped off toward her cubs.

Ollikut crawled down off the roof and walked into the cabin. From one look he could tell it would take a heap of cleaning and repair before anyone could use it again. He didn't think the trapper would return after that episode anyway.

Salvaging what he could and collecting his beaver hides Ollikut headed for home. The day had been quite profitable after all.

Later, reports came back with visitors from Lapwai of a big Indian with a bear that had attacked and almost killed a trapper. The Wallowa was not bothered much after that by trappers. Ollikut was pleased that the trapper had not been killed and was full of laughter about the stories of the big Indian with the bear. Thinking back, however, he decided next time to try another way. That bear had gotten too close and if he had tripped just once, it would not be he who laughed but the trapper.

Chapter 14

THE PASSING OF THE OLD CHIEF

Old Chief Joseph had lived a long, useful life. He was now quite old and weak. He kept getting weaker and his eyesight was failing him. He knew it was about the end of his years during the winter of 1871. His life had been filled with joy and excitement. Adventure had walked with him through the years. He had two strong, wise sons and one daughter with him now. They were married and happy. His other children were older and lived in other parts of the Nez Perce Country. The Chief had lived a full and fruitful life. What more could a man ask. As his days grew very short he called his sons to his bedside.

Joseph, the oldest, went in first and sat down next to his father. Ollikut followed and sat next to his father on the other side.

"My sons, I am proud of you both. Our people need the qualities in each of you to guide them through the troublesome years ahead. Joseph, your peaceful ways and your ability to persuade will aid you in maintaining the peace between our people and the whites. I counsel you to follow your heart tempered with the thoughts of your mind," he advised.

"Ollikut, you have walked in peace even though you were angered by the actions of the whites. Always remember to follow your mind tempered by your heart."

"You both must be wise and all knowing. You must guide our people out of danger. Never fight unless you must. But the day will come when words alone will not save our Wallowa."

"My sons, my body is returning to mother earth, and my spirit is going very soon to see the Great Spirit Chief. When I am gone, think of your country. You are the chiefs of these people. They look to you to guide them. Always remember that your father never sold his country."

"You must stop your ears whenever you are asked to sign a treaty selling your home. Now the white men are all around you. They have their eyes on this land. My sons, never forget my dying words. This country holds your father's body. Never sell the bones of your father and your mother."

With this, Old Chief Joseph passed to the spirit land he had often thought of and contemplated its mysteries. He knew he would be with his old friends and counsel with the Great Spirit. His death was an end to an era of Nez Perce history.

His widows, dressed in soiled and tattered clothing, mourned for him. They cut off their long braids and threw them into the fire. The wailing and mourning was very sad and very loud.

After two days of lying in state, dressed in his finest clothes, he was tightly wrapped in a buffalo hide and laid upon poles. Four strong warriors carried the body to the grave site.

The Dreamer was asked to say a few words of praise for the dead chief. Smohalla, in his usual eloquent manner, eulogized the chief in such a way that left not a dry eye.

At the conclusion of the Dreamer's speech the body was lowered into the grave and the grave was covered with poles. Rocks were placed on the poles. Over the rocks, dirt and sod were placed. Thorny brush was then stuck in among the rocks. This was all to prevent coyotes or other predators from digging it up. After the grave was covered, a favorite horse of the Chief's was killed next to his grave. This was so he would have a fine horse to ride in the spirit land. Each year after that, another good horse would be killed by his grave so that he would always have a fresh horse.

The Old Chief's wives moved his lodge to a new place so the ghost would not haunt it. They continued mourning for a month. At the end of the month a feast was held. There was happiness and gaiety. During the feast the personal belongings of the Chief were given away to relatives and friends.

Ollikut and Joseph both missed their father. He had been a fountain of knowledge for them. His strength had protected them in battle as well as at the treaty councils. His eyes had seen the old, the new and ever changing world while the two sons had only known the new life with the white man's presence. Neither of them could remember before the Spaulding mission was opened.

Now it was up to them to lead, guide and direct their people as their father would have had he still lived. They both wanted peace but, Ollikut wondered, peace at what price? He felt honor bound to stay in the Wallowa.

Old Joseph did not live long enough to see his marriage blessing to Ollikut and Wetatonmi come true. He had blessed them that they might have a son, and they did. This time neither Ollikut nor Wetatonmi had a hard time finding a name for him as they had their horses. They called him Young Ollikut. They were both very proud of this fine son. They were happy he would have the wide-open country in the Wallowa to grow up in.

This boy was going to learn to hunt and fish and be a man that other men would be proud to follow. Ollikut was sad in one way, though, for he wished his young son would have had the tutoring of his grandfather. Old Joseph could have taught him so much. It was the custom for the older relatives to teach the young the arts of hunting and camping and to tell them stories of the olden days before the white man.

Ollikut could remember his grandfather's stories still, but his grandfather had died before Ollikut could hunt. His uncle had taught him how to break horses. His father had spent time with him during hunting and fishing trips to show him the best ways to do things.

Ollikut vowed to take the time to teach his young son, as he grew up, how to be the man his grandfather would have wanted him to be. There was no better place to teach him, Ollikut thought, than in the Wallowa.

Time passed quite rapidly, and the baby grew into a toddler. Ollikut spent many hours with him in the evenings playing and giving him rides on the horses. Even at two, Young Ollikut was showing signs of enjoying the horses and the rides in the hills. His mother would take him for rides almost every day. She didn't want to stop riding just because she had a baby to take care of. He learned to fall asleep from the rocking of the horse. Wetatonmi was very proud of her young son also. She took the best care of him and he grew strong.

More and more whites were moving into the Wallowa every summer. Ollikut had many run-ins with them. He had been very careful to use only words, not weapons, against these enemies. Many times the climate for bloodshed was there, but it was the Indian and not the white that withdrew. Joseph had counseled his people that bloodshed would only bring more bloodshed.

In early spring of 1873, a council was called to talk the non-treaty Indians into leaving the Wallowa and moving onto the Lapwai reservation. The climate was cordial. Both sides knew that the results of this meeting could be very important for each side in its own way.

Joseph asked Ollikut to sit with him in the council. Even though Joseph was considered the civil leader of the band, he wanted Ollikut's wisdom to help guide him. This was the first time Joseph had the opportunity to represent his people in council with the white man.

The meeting was set up by the Indian agent. He was told to find a way of settling the white settlers in the Wallowa in a peaceful manner. Governor L.F. Grover had asked that this be accomplished with all possible haste.

Realizing what his father had said on his death bed, and with Ollikut at his right arm, Joseph said, "I came to this council hoping that we could save blood. The white man has no right to come here and take our country. We have never accepted any presents from the Government. Neither Lawyer nor any other chief had authority to sell this land. It has always belonged to my people. It came unclouded to them from our fathers, and we will defend this land as long as a drop of Indian blood warms the hearts of our men."

Joseph told of the problems of the 1863 treaty and said that his people were still living up to the 1855 treaty they signed. After much talking back and forth, the commissioners stood up and looked straight at Joseph.

"Chief, you have made a good argument why we should not let the white man move onto the Wallowa. Those that are there should be bought out by the government and moved elsewhere. This is my recommendation," said the commissioner.

This pleased Ollikut and Joseph. It was their first victory against the white man and it had cost no blood. As they rode home they laughed and joked. This was a very happy moment for them both. They were becoming friends instead of rivals.

On June 16, 1873, President Grant issued an executive order withdrawing the Wallowa Valley from settlement as public domain. This was good news and the people of the Wallowa rejoiced. They felt their worries were over. Now they could just think about raising horses and cattle with an occasional buffalo trip thrown in for excitement.

Governor Grover persistently pleaded with President Grant to open the Wallowa. Five hundred Indians did not need more than a million acres of land. So, on June 10, 1875, the 1873 order was revoked by the President. The Wallowa was again open for settling by the whites. The Governor once again ordered the Commissioners of Indian Affairs to see that the non-treaty Nez Perce were placed on the Lapwai reservation as soon as possible.

The change in the President's mind and words upset Ollikut greatly. He could not understand how a great man like the President could speak right one day and wrong the next. What could they believe from any white man if the President could not be trusted to keep his word? A white man's word had little value to Ollikut.

Joseph called a council of the non-treaty Nez Perce for three suns hence. He knew all these people needed to understand the gravity of the situation.

"My people, I have studied the treaty and the President's orders. We have been ordered to move and we have no other course to take. There are too many soldiers and whites to fight. They have more people and they will bring even more. They will outnumber us greatly."

The Dreamer spoke up and said, "I have been receiving revelations from the Great Spirit He has told me we must not move. He said the whites would not start war because they knew how many whites would die. We must stay where we are," the Dreamer advised.

"Maybe the Dreamer is right. I know that the whites are afraid of our repeater rifles and fast horses. Joseph, let us stay as long as we can without war," Ollikut said.

Chapter 15

MOVE OR ELSE

By 1875 a dozen white families had settled in the Wallowa. These settlers were grassing cattle on the horse pastures of the Nez Perce. They also cut the meadows and put up hay. This took even more feed from the horse herds. This encroachment of settlers along with the miners caused friction. As this friction increased, the settlers began demanding the Army enforce the 1863 treaty.

About this time a new agent by the name of John B. Monteith arrived at Lapwai. He was a stern man with little outward emotion. The treaty Nez Perce got along with this new agent. Because of the added paper work and worry brought on by the non-treaty Nez Perce living off the Lapwai reservation, Monteith was not very tactful when dealing with them.

Meeting Ollikut in the trading post, Monteith assumed he was Joseph. "I must inform you how important it is that you move onto the Lapwai reservation. I can assure you there will be food and goods given to your people when you do move."

"I will not, and my people will not, we do not need your goods. We have plenty, we are content and happy. If the white man will let us alone, we will be peaceful."

"But you have more land than you need and the white settlers are crowded for pasture."

"The Lapwai reservation is too small for so many people with all our stock," Ollikut insisted.

"But by giving up your spotted horses you would have much less stock. Once you move onto the reservation and start farming, you will have no need for the fast horses," said Monteith.

"You can keep your presents and we will keep our horses," replied Ollikut. "We can go to your towns and pay for all we need. We have plenty of horses and cattle to sell. We won't accept any help from you. We are free. We can go where we please. Our fathers were born in the Wallowa. Here they lived, and here they died. Here are their graves. We will never leave them."

Monteith was very upset but could see he was getting nowhere. "We will see if you will leave or not," he said bitterly and departed from the trading post.

Within a month Monteith had obtained authority to stop all hunting parties leaving for the buffalo country to the east. He maintained that the non-treaty or "wild" Indians, as he called them, talked their friends among the treaty Indians to go hunting with them which caused many problems in their farming program. Despite that, Monteith let the situation drag on for almost two years.

The non-treaty Indians became even more hostile with Monteith when he tried to stop them from going to the buffalo country. He told them that he had the authority to use the U.S. Cavalry to stop them if necessary. He had been told about the last encounter with the Cavalry. He thought better than to use force with these Indians.

In relating the situation to General O.O. Howard, he said, "I might as well talk to the wind as talk to the non-treaties."

Howard told him to tell Chief Joseph he had until April 1, 1877, to move onto the reservation peacefully.

Monteith summoned Joseph to come to his office. He informed Joseph of the final date to move or troops would be used. Joseph was very concerned and finally decided there should be a meeting with General Howard before a course of action could be made. General Howard agreed to the meeting. The date was to be May 1, 1877, at Umatilla. This bought the Nez Perce another month.

Instead of coming himself, General Howard sent Lieutenant Boyle, a young looking man. Hearing this, Joseph sent Ollikut. Boyle was an egotistical, over-bearing young officer. He started telling Ollikut what he would do, or else. Ollikut was not permitted to discuss the situation. Finally Ollikut said, "I will not talk to a boy about such important matters as the land of my people." With this he departed.

Another meeting was set for May 8 at Walla Walla. Ollikut again went in Joseph's place. This time Joseph had intended to go but became ill and could not make the journey. Ollikut was impressed with one-arm Howard. He was a large man with white hair and beard. Having a glorious career in the Civil War, he had been promoted to a Brigadier General. Howard was equally impressed with the beautiful specimen of a man he saw in Ollikut. Howard told his officers afterward that he was very impressed with the way Ollikut conducted himself but was very sorry that they could not see eye to eye on anything more important than the weather.

It was not a good meeting. Howard would not reconsider the decision to move all non-treaty Nez Perce onto the reservation. Ollikut would not acknowledge that the non-treaty group had sold their land. Therefore, Howard had no right to move them. The meeting ended in an agreement for another meeting May 15 in Lapwai.

The next meeting was to include White Bird and Looking Glass as well as Joseph and Ollikut. The latter two arrived one day late, as usual, but found White Bird and Looking Glass had not yet arrived. General Howard came to them and told them he could not wait, the meeting must begin.

"This time all will be present when decisions are made. We cannot say yes or no for White Bird or Looking Glass. They must say what will be for their people," Ollikut said.

Howard fumed and fussed but to no avail.

The next day White Bird and Looking Glass arrived. They had been held up because of deep snow over some of the trail. They were not concerned with General Howard's rude comments about being late for they had made as good time as they could considering the trail's condition.

Monteith first gave a speech about why the non-treaty Nez Perce had to move to the reservation.

"And if you don't come on the reservation of your own will, my soldiers will put you there," Howard said.

This did not sit well with any of the Indians. They did not like war spoken of at a peace meeting.

It was now Ollikut's turn to speak. By now he was quite upset and could see the mood of the meeting. Rising, he said, "If we ever owned the land we own it still for we never sold it. In the treaty councils the commissioners have claimed that our country had been sold to the Government. Suppose a white man should come to me and say, 'Ollikut, I like your horses and I want to buy them.' I say to him, 'No, my horses suit me. I will not sell them.' Then he goes to my neighbor and says to him, 'Ollikut has some good horses. I want to buy them but he refuses to sell.' My neighbor answers, 'Pay me the money and I will sell you his horses.' The white man returns to me and says, Ollikut, I have bought your horses and you must let me have them. If we sold our lands to the

Government, this is the way they were bought.'"

Howard disagreed saying, "An alliance or coalition of all Nez Perce was formed prior to 1863 that had the authority to act for all the Nez Perce. Under this alliance six chiefs had signed in agreement with the treaty which made it binding on all Nez Perce."

Ollikut jumped up and said, "Yes, this was the treaty of thieves. We will not be bound by our cowardly people who sold what was not theirs to sell."

This exchange went on for two days, getting nowhere.

On the third day Monteith gave the same speech for the third time, of how the non-treaty Nez Perce must move to the reservation. This day was slightly different than the previous two days in as much as the Dreamer had arrived and was attending.

Howard, expecting trouble because he planned to force the issue, had moved the meeting to within one hundred fifty steps of the guard house.

After Monteith's spoke, the Dreamer stood up.

"The land belongs to the Great Spirit and no man can tell another where to live or how to live. The bones of the dead are buried on this land. These people have the right to the land and have promised, to the dead, never to leave their graves for the white man to plow up."

Howard could only take so much of this then he told Smohalla to stop and sit down.

"Is this not a council where both sides can say what they feel, or is it only you who says what will be? I will not be still! These things are true and you must listen to them, Smohalla shouted. Howard ordered the guards to take Smohalla to the guard house. With this action the Chiefs all wanted to go to their knives and kill them all. Joseph counseled them to be patient and told Smohalla to go along peacefully. This ended the meeting.

Joseph could see that Howard was willing and able to use force to get his way. He counseled the other chiefs that there should be no war because they could not win. All it would bring would be sorrow. Looking Glass finally agreed. White Bird and Ollikut were not at all convinced that this was the thing to do, but finally agreed that they would go along with it for now.

That night the non-treaty Chiefs met in council to discuss the bleak situation. Joseph was set on peace at any price. Ollikut and White Bird did not agree. They were not going to be trapped on a reservation.

White Bird suggested traveling north to live with Sitting Bull's people in the Grand Mother's Country, Canada. He felt if they all went together they could make the trip safely.

Ollikut did not want to leave the Wallowa. Going north still meant leaving the Wallowa to the white man. He wanted to stay and fight for the Wallowa as his father had counseled.

This council went on for hours. Joseph was firm about going onto the reservation with no fighting. Looking Glass was luke warm about what direction to take. He finally threw in with Joseph, as this was the simplest way.

Ollikut did not want to leave his brother and his people. He finally agreed to try the reservation but cautioned if it was bad he would run away to the north.

White Bird knew he couldn't fight the white men with his small band of Nez Perce. He wanted to go north but didn't want to chance going through the northern Indian country with a small band for he feared the Indians to the north even more than the white man. Finally, he too decided to try the reservation.

The next morning the Chiefs told General Howard they would look at the possible sites on the reservation. This put the General in a new frame of mind. He rode with them for the next two days while they looked for possible sites for their new homes.

At the end of the second day, General Howard told each chief when he must be on the reservation. Because Joseph and Ollikut had been the trouble leaders, in his mind, Howard told them they had only until June 15 to be on the reservation. He gave White Bird until August 15 and Looking Glass did not have to be there until September 1st of that year. Even though the latter two would have farther to come, they did not have to cross the Snake River.

To cross the Snake River in June was like committing suicide. Joseph told Howard they needed more time, but Monteith counseled Howard not to back down now or they would end up with more talks and time wasted. Howard had now made up his mind and that was that.

Ollikut and White Bird both knew the Dreamer was being held in the guard house unfairly.

"Will you go with me to free Smohalla?" White Bird asked Ollikut.

"We have an obligation to set him free. He was not wrong to talk about things that are true," Ollikut replied.

"How are we going to do this deed?" White Bird questioned.

"I think it would be better if only I go to the fort," Ollikut responded. "One Indian dressed in white man's clothes would be less noticed. I will get there about dark. Then the night will hide me."

"I want to go. I could hold the horses outside the fort while you free him," White Bird insisted.

That afternoon they rode to the cabins near the fort. Having buildings by the fort made it easy to get close.

White Bird held the horses while Ollikut, dressed in white man's clothes, slipped over the fort wall at the stable area. This area was not guarded.

Working his way through, the horses gave him cover. Once past the horses he had to walk openly toward the guard house. It was off to the side of the barracks which gave him cover to reach the guard house.

Only one guard was in front. Ollikut came up the side of the guard house and quickly stepped next to the guard. It took him by surprise. Ollikut quickly hit him with a swift blow just below the center of the ribs. The force pushed the stomach hard into the lungs. This caused him to pass out immediately.

Ollikut grabbed him by the shoulders and pulled him out of sight. Grabbing the keys, Ollikut slipped around and quickly opened the door.

"I have been waiting for you Ollikut. My spirit flew to you. I sent it two days ago. How come it took you so long?"

"Tell your spirit friend to help us get out of here without being shot."

Slipping out the door, they retraced Ollikut's path to the wall. The Dreamer, being short, had to stand on Ollikut's shoulders to get over the wall. Just then, he heard the guard screaming for help.

Jumping up, Ollikut caught the top rail on the wall, swung over and dropped down to the ground. A few steps and he was at Henawit's side. The Dreamer had already mounted. Holding Henawit's mane, Ollikut let him start running. One bounce on the ground and he was astride Henawit.

The guard on the wall saw them as they cleared the cabin they were using for cover. He was firing as fast as his repeater would fire. The bullets were flying past them, but the guard was not aiming well. It was so dark he couldn't see his front sight.

It was light enough for the guard to see the white on Henawit's rump. He had seen that horse before and reported his observation to the night officer in charge.

The three slipped into the darkness and were not followed. Once they were clear of town, Ollikut advised Smohalla that his best escape would be to travel south to the Sioux.

The next morning, Monteith, accompanied by four soldiers, rode into the Wallowa. They approached Joseph first.

"We have a witness that saw Ollikut break the Dreamer out of jail. He recognized his horse. We intend to arrest him. We will search for the Dreamer while you get Ollikut."

Chief Joseph went to Ollikut's tepee.

"Did you ride to Fort Lapwai last night and free the Dreamer?"

"I did go out for a ride last night, but surely I wouldn't attempt freeing the Dreamer amongst all those soldiers."

"I'm sure glad. They are here to arrest you."

Monteith and the soldiers pulled up in front of Ollikut's lodge.

"We are arresting you for freeing the Dreamer last night."

"You must have the wrong man. I was riding in the hills last evening."

"The guard recognized the horse you rode. That's enough to charge you on."

"Let's walk up to my horse herd and you can show me which horse I was riding."

It was a short walk to Ollikut's pasture. As they approached, a spotted horse came out of the trees.

"That's the horse," the guard shouted.

Behind that horse came another with the big, white rump. Then another. Soon there were six horses with white, spotted rumps.

"Now, which horse was I riding?"

"Well, I'm not sure. They all look alike."

As they were walking back to camp White Bird rode up on another white, blanketed, spotted horse.

"What's the problem?" White Bird questioned.

"Someone helped the Dreamer escape last night and we think it was Ollikut," Monteith said.

"It couldn't have been Ollikut. He was with me riding in the hills last night."

"You didn't find the Dreamer. Your guard couldn't pick out the horse he saw and White Bird was with Ollikut last night. It doesn't look like you have any evidence it was Ollikut," Joseph said.

With that, the riders left camp.

"You and White Bird better ride closer to camp next time so more people can see you," Joseph cautioned, knowing full well no one else would have attempted such a dangerous feat.

After hearing the news of Howard's edict, Joseph called all the people together and began to speak.

"For many years I have hunted in these groves and fished in the stream. For many years I have worshipped on this ground as my father did and his father did before him. Through these groves and over the plateaus our fathers roamed. By them this land was left unto us as a great heritage forever. No one is more attached to his home than myself. Not one among you is more grieved to leave it. But the time is near at hand when we of the Wallowa will have to leave the land of our birth and find a home of the white man's choosing. The white men of the east, whose numbers are like the sands of the sea, will overrun and take possession of our country. They will build houses and villages all over the land, and their domain will extend from sea to sea."

"In my boyhood days I have chased the antelope across the prairies and hunted the elk in the groves. But, where are they now? Long since they have drawn afar. The approach of the white man has frightened them away. The deer will go next and with them the sons of the forest."

"Resistance to the aggression of the whites is useless. War is wicked and would result in our ruin. Therefore, let us submit to our fate. Return not evil for evil as this would offend the Great Spirit and surely bring ruin upon us. The time is near when our race will become extinct and nothing will be left to show the world that we ever did exist, but this I do know, the heart within my breast has taught me the will of the Great Spirit, and now tells me good people will be rewarded and bad ones punished."

"My friends, do not listen to those that counsel you to war. Do not dirty your hands in human blood. Such is the work of the evil one and will only lead to blood upon all our heads."

It did not take much discussion before the elders realized there was no other way. They realized that war would not be the answer but an end for their people. The vote was taken and the decision was made that all would go in peace to the Lapwai area to be given 20 acre plots to farm.

In closing Chief Joseph said, "The many moons and sunny days we have lived here will long be remembered by us. The Great Spirit has smiled upon us and made us glad for living here. But we have agreed to go. Let us go in peace."

It was hard for the people to realize that they must move and even harder to think of crossing the Snake River with all the families and stock in the middle of June. Ollikut helped Joseph by telling the young warriors there was nothing else that could have been done. He told them of the Dreamer being put in the guard house and the many soldiers standing around with their rifles ready.

With this the people all agreed on what must be done. Now the stock had to be gathered and preparations for moving made. The young men and boys were sent out to gather the stock. This was a big job when there were one million acres to cover by about 100 riders. After two weeks, most of the stock close in had been collected. Having so much stock they really couldn't know how much was missing, but they knew they had missed quite a number of horses in the higher country.

It was decided to cross the Snake River and camp for a few days in White Bird Canyon before going on to the reservation.

The next morning Ollikut stood for a few moments with Wetatonmi and Young Ollikut looking at the beautiful Wallowa Valley and the mountains to the south. Turning to Wetatonmi he said, "Last night I saw the sun set for the last time, and its light shown upon the tree tops and the land and the water that I may never look upon again. My only hope is that someday our son can return to this valley in peace after all the bitterness between the whites and Indians has faded."

Crossing the Snake River was no easy matter. The women and children with all their belongings were taken across in buffalo bowl rafts first. The rafts were made of willows for a frame with a buffalo hide covering. The willows were bowed up and other willows fastened around the top to make a long oval raft about one and a half feet deep. These rafts could carry quite a bit of weight. A rope was tied to each of four corners and a brave on horseback held each rope. In this way, the raft was guided and pulled by the swimming horses across the fast running river.

The first day was devoted to getting the people across. Luckily, not one was lost. They had the great spotted horses to thank for this feat.

Ollikut had been very worried about the crossing. He had crossed the Snake River many times, but always tried to go early in the spring before the heavy runoff or in the summer when the river was lower. Even then it was not an easy task for a horse had to swim part of the way. With the high, muddy water it was very dangerous for a man, let alone the women and children. He was so thankful that the people were all across.

The next day might be more costly, he knew, because the mares had new colts and the cows had their calves. It took strong legs for such a crossing and he was afraid they would lose the young and the old stock.

His fears were soon a reality as the next day drew to a close. They had lost 900 horses, besides all the colts. All of the calves and many cattle were swept downstream. Many of the animals got out downstream, but they were miles down the river in the steep canyons. There was no time to collect them and, in some cases, no way to get to them from upstream.

That night they rested and dried their wet belongings. Some of the men had made over a dozen trips across the river that day. They had used up many horses and they were tired too.

Getting a late start the next morning, they moved the remaining cattle and horses up to the Salmon River. The stock needed a rest before crossing and the feed was good so they left them there and continued to rendezvous with White Bird for a few days prior to going to the reservation.

It was now June 12 and Ollikut realized there were only three more days of freedom before they would have to submit to the agent's rules and regulations. No more buffalo hunts would be permitted. The only way he would be able to leave the reservation was to request a pass, and it had to be for a good reason. He thought back to Young Timothy and how he had felt sorry for him. Now he was going to be bound by the same laws. He would also be required to farm for a living. The thought of the changes demanded in his life made him sick inside. Wetatonmi was also broken-hearted to think they could no longer live a free life. They had plenty of store bought goods and she had enjoyed these past years living in the Wallowa. She had learned to love it as much as Ollikut. Their son, Young Ollikut, found life in the Wallowa fun and exciting. He was growing up with the ability to ride and play in the wide open country. There were no fields he could not ride in or fences for his horse to get caught in. At six, he was a fine young boy that Ollikut and Wetatonmi were very proud of. They did not like the idea of him growing up in Lapwai with the young treaty Indians and being sent to school and church with them. They wanted him to learn the ways of his people, not the white man's ways of telling lies and fighting over religious matters. This was not the way they had dreamed Young Ollikut would be raised. The thought of leaving the reservation had been in both of their minds. They had talked of going north as soon as things became possible. They thought they might slip off the reservation unnoticed and be in Canada before they were missed.

Chapter 16
CRAZY YOUNG WARRIORS

At the rendezvous were White Bird's band, Joseph's people and another 300 Indians from the Palouse and the other bands of Indians that felt the same way about their freedom. They, too, were being forced from their birth lands onto reservations at Walla Walla and Umatilla.

The white settlers had observed Indians coming into the area for the past week. They were afraid it meant war, and many families moved into town to wait until they knew the Indians were safely on the reservation. Some stayed, thinking there would be no fight, while others were friends with the Indians and did not fear for their safety.

With over six hundred Indians at the rendezvous there were games of all kinds. Some were gambling games while others were feats of strength. Yet, others were horseback games and competition. These Ollikut liked best. He never missed a chance to prove the power and skill of his great stallion, Henawit. This was no exception. He joined in the races and won each time. There was no horse in the camp that could outrun or out-maneuver Henawit. This was the sire of his many fine horses which caused most of his friends and even his enemies to be jealous. They knew Henawit was a Spirit horse and his offspring were some of the greatest of all the spotted horses.

As the day was ending Joseph came to Ollikut and asked if he would go back to the cattle herd with him to get fresh meat for their people. Ollikut asked Watatonmi to go and Joseph took his daughter, Running Spring. They were also accompanied by two other braves to help lead the twelve packhorses and help with the butchering. They spent the next day killing and butchering the cattle. They packed the twelve horses with the fresh meat and started back across the Salmon.

They had no more reached the east bank of the Salmon River when a messenger came with bad news. Some of White Bird's braves had gone on a killing spree and left four white men dead and another wounded in their path of violence the previous evening. Joseph was afraid this might happen and had counseled White Bird to control his young men. They all hurried back to camp to get more details.

When they arrived in camp Joseph had still another problem. His wife had given premature birth to a baby girl while he was gone. She was still sometime away, they thought, but the rough trip across the Snake River must have caused the baby to come early. They were both okay but very weak. The meat would give them strength. They would be able to travel soon, Joseph thought. Then the thought also came to him that his people would be blamed for these killings because he was the one most thought of as the spokesman for the non-treaty Nez Perce. He must find out what had happened and try to talk to General Howard and stop any more killing, he decided.

Meeting White Bird, he asked, "What happened yesterday?"

"The night before the killings, Wahtitats, Red Moccasin and Spotted Necklace were riding through the camp shooting and shouting. They rode over some roots that the Dreamer's wife had set out to dry. This made the Dreamer's wife even more angry than she already was. Jumping up, she called out to Wahtitats to use his energy to avenge the death of his father, Eagle Robes, by the white man's hands rather than playing games and destroying her work. This made Wahtitats very upset because he had wanted to avenge his father's death but had promised his father as he lay dying that he would not kill Larry Ott, his father's killer. As you know, his father had befriended Ott and allowed him to stay on Indian land and raise a small farm. When Ott fenced Wahtitat's father's garden land, the old Indian asked him to leave, but instead Ott shot Eagle Robes. Later that day he died," White Bird informed Joseph.

"Wahtitats and his friends rode off that night to look for Larry Ott but could not find him. The next morning they found Richard Divine, an Indian hater, and killed him. Then they killed Henry Elfers. There were women in the Elfer's homestead, but they were not hurt. Later in the day they crossed paths with Robert Blank and Henry Beckrage and killed them. Henry Beckrage had a fast race horse that was winning races around the area. They took the horse and sent Spotted Necklace back to camp on him to prove to the people that his story was true."

"Spotted Necklace told of the vision Wahtitats had some months before but had not known what to do. It was from the Great Spirit and was reported in this way."

"You, Wahtitats, shall avenge the death of your father and appease his spirit. Your feet shall be as swift as the forked lightning. Your arm shall be as the thunderbolt, and your soul fearless."

"Today you saw a deer bounding through the forest. He was lively in strength and beauty and fleeter than the winds. Suddenly the hunter crossed his path and an arrow entered the deer's heart. I led you to the spot and bade you look at the dying animal. The warm blood that flowed from the wound grew dark and chill. He was stiff and cold and his beauty had departed. Such is death, and such was the death of your father."

"Time rolls on without ceasing. The winter passes quickly away and spring is here again. You shall soon glory in the strength of your manhood and your enemies shall hear your name and tremble," White Bird related.

When Spotted Necklace's story was told, White Bird asked Joseph and Ollikut what they thought should be done.

"I would give my life if I could undo the killings of the white men yesterday. I blame our young men and I blame the white man," Joseph paused . . . "My enemies among the white men will blame me for the killings. I am not to blame."

Ollikut broke in, "Although I do not justify them, I remember all the insults I have endured and my blood was on fire. Still I would advise taking our people to buffalo country without a fight, if possible."

Chief Joseph's and Ollikut's half-brothers, were on their way home from the buffalo country with their band. A messenger was sent to tell them of the situation before they were attacked by outraged settlers.

Ollikut was the leader of the warriors and because of this he became the commander of his band for the withdrawal. Joseph's responsibility was to stay with the women and children and see to their safety if any fighting occurred.

That night Ollikut directed their people to pack for a long trip to the buffalo country. The next morning at first light they departed to reclaim their stock and move toward Montana.

Captain Perry, along with 99 troopers, was sent by General

Howard to try to obtain a meeting with Joseph and Ollikut to find out what had gone wrong. Howard's superiors had all the bad public opinion they could stand from their handling of Crazy Horse the year before. They did not want another Indian war. Perry was told, "Do not fight unless you find it completely necessary."

Before attempting to enforce the 1863 treaty, General Howard wanted a clear assessment of that treaty.

In the spring of 1877, Major H. Clay Wood, General Howard's very capable adjutant at the Headquarters of the Department of the Columbia, made a study of the 1863 treaty problem of which he stated:

"In my opinion the non-treaty Nez Perce cannot in law be regarded as bound by the treaty of 1863 and in so far as it attempts to deprive them of a right to occupancy of any land its provisions are null and void. The extinguishment of their title of occupancy contemplated by this treaty is imperfect and incomplete."

Howard read this assessment and realized he really didn't have the legality to force the non-treaty Nez Perce off their land. Yet, his supervisors were demanding he do just that. He didn't want any bloodshed. He informed all his subordinates not to start any military action against the non-treaty people.

On Perry's arrival in the area he found a volunteer company led by a former Confederate Major, "Ad" Chapman, ready to go to battle. Perry was new to Indian fighting and would not be easily coerced into attacking the Indians.

"One hit and we can smash the heathens," the Major told Captain Perry.

While Ollikut had moved back across the Salmon to the

cattle and horses, some of White Bird's warriors had gone on another killing spree. This time sixteen whites were dead, some of them women and children. Although Joseph's band had no hand in this, they were still non-treaty Indians and the main group Perry was after.

Within three hours Perry and the volunteers were on their way to intercept what they thought was a small band of Indians. News of their arrival preceded them for Ollikut had sent scouts out so they wouldn't be taken by surprise. Joseph had counseled to parley, if possible, and Ollikut agreed.

Upon sighting the Indians, Perry stopped and sent Captain John, a Nez Perce scout, to request a parley with Joseph and Ollikut. The parley was set up but without Joseph because he was not with this group. Ollikut and four other men rode out to meet them. Perry and Lieutenant Theller, accompanied by Ad Chapman, started towards them. When the two groups were about a hundred yards apart Ad Chapman lifted his rifle and fired. The shot was intended for Ollikut as they thought it was Joseph they were parleying with. It whizzed by Ollikut's arm and hit Wittewitli Honlies (Mean Person) in the chest and killed him instantly. Perry was upset but there was no time for talking now. It was a fight he would get and he knew it. Chapman wanted it that way. He did not want to see the red devils talk their way out of this one.

Ollikut could see there was no chance for talking. The volunteers had come to fight. He had twenty of his warriors put on their big, red blanket coats. With the men behind him, Ollikut got as close as possible to the line of volunteers. They kept riding forward towards Ollikut's position. When they were within two hundred yards, Ollikut and his warriors rode straight for the volunteers. The red coats were flapping in the wind and the Indians were shooting and yelling. All the commotion unnerved the volunteers; they broke and ran. This left the troops open to fire. Otstotpoo (Fire Body), and Old Man made good shots and killed the bugler, Trumpeteer John Joes. He was the first soldier to die in the Nez Perce war, he wouldn't be the last.

Another group of Indians led by Yellow Wolf came from their left flank. Ollikut closed in and they started to fire. These were fresh troops that had not been in battle with Indians before. They were filled with the thoughts of Crazy Horse's treatment of Custer and his troops. The first thing Perry knew, his command had been cut in two. Ollikut had ridden right through the center of his line. Perry could see that great spotted horse of Ollikut's streaking through. One of his lieutenants and fifteen men were cut off. After a short fight with Ollikut's men, they were all killed. The battle raged on, but the volunteers had scattered and were heading back to town. Perry and his men finally found a hole in Ollikut's line of fire and rode for town. Ollikut gave pursuit for a short distance, then withdrew.

In all, Perry lost Lieutenant Theller and thirty-three enlisted men. He also lost two pack mules loaded with ammunition, over sixty repeating rifles and many pistols. These weapons were retrieved by Ollikut and his warriors. He had only three men wounded, plus the one killed by Chapman.

Ollikut knew this was a short-lived victory. Other soldiers would come soon and there would be more fighting. They had to move quickly. Returning to camp he sent a rider around to tell the people to prepare for another move. They would have to take their cattle, horses and all their belongings with them. This would not be a fast retreat, but they could move faster than they might have with the little calves and colts that were lost in the Snake River.

Crossing to the south side of the Salmon River at Horseshoe Bend, they headed up the mountains towards Montana. By noon they met Young Chief and his people coming back from buffalo hunting. After telling Young Chief of the fighting and killing, he agreed to join them. White Bird, Looking Glass and the rest of the non-treaty Indians also joined the group at this stop. They all realized they must run or be killed after the killing the young men had done. Altogether there were about 750 Indians and over four thousand horses. They took some cattle and all of their belongings. They realized they might never see the Nez Perce country again. From here they moved with haste to the Clearwater Country.

Joseph's wife and baby were quite sick from the moves and the bouncing around on the horses. Wetatonmi had been trying to take care of the baby, but with the mother weak and tired, the baby was not getting enough milk and was showing the effects of the elements.

Howard prepared a forced march as soon as he received word of Perry's fiasco. Within three days he had crossed the Salmon and was on the trail of the Nez Perce. He knew he was close so he sent out an advanced party accompanied by James Reuben, a Christian Nez Perce scout.

Upon coming across Looking Glass' camp, Reuben called out, "You cowardly people, come over here. We will have a war."

Looking Glass was angered, "You call us cowards when we fight for our homes, our women, our children. We run so there will be no more war. It is you who are the cowards hiding behind the soldiers."

Looking Glass' camp was now surrounded by the little group of soldiers. He was told to surrender. The Lieutenant in charge felt sure there would be no fight when he had the camp surrounded. He had, however, spread his men too thin. Looking Glass and a few warriors dashed to the cover of the trees and slowly, with just their bows and arrows, disarmed the soldiers and sent those still able running back to Howard. Now Looking Glass had some guns and ammunition.

Howard was becoming outraged over the defeats his men were taking. He had cannons and plenty of supplies so he felt confident he could soon overtake and subdue these renegades. They had horses, cattle and families to move.

After Looking Glass's encounter, Ollikut moved the group to the banks of the Clearwater River where they made James Lawyer, son of Chief Lawyer, ferry them across the Clearwater in his large boat. It took much time to get everyone across. They forded the river with the horses and cattle. Ollikut knew Howard would try to use this same boat to cross after them. Once all the people and supplies were on the other side, he ordered the boat sunk. This would mean Howard would have to ford the river.

It took Howard a whole day to build rafts for his cannons and ammunition that was packed on the 23 mules he had brought. As he was attempting the crossing, Ollikut and a few warriors started firing from the other bank. The commotion was too much. One after another, rafts got away from the soldiers until they had only one raft of ammunition when they reached the other side. Many of the mules had been carried down river and much of their provisions lost.

Ollikut did not want to make a fight there, but rather just upset Howard's chances of following them. This he had done very nicely. Without food or ammunition there was no possibility of Howard following them farther at this time.

Confident their worries were over for awhile, Ollikut let the people rest for three days and hoped that Joseph's wife and baby would get better. This was not the case, however, for all that Wetatonmi had done for the baby was in vain. On the third day the baby died. Joseph's wife was still very sick. Joseph spent most of his time at camp with her and helped the others get ready for the next move. Someone had to be responsible for their safety and he was their civil leader.

Howard had thought ahead about supplies and had ordered a supply company with 35 mules to follow him the next day. With the day's travel he lost building the rafts, the supply company had just about time to catch him. With this in mind he sent scouts out to find it and get it across the Clearwater at the most shallow part. This was done, and within three days Howard was prepared to march again.

Ollikut had left scouts to watch the soldier's movements. He was becoming very uneasy with the soldiers camping rather than returning to the fort. When he heard of the new supplies coming, he knew they were in for a fight. It was strange, he thought, how now he and his people were thought of as savages, heathens and killers of the worst kind when his father had told him that Captain Bonneville had praised them for being so industrious, kind and peace-loving. Had they really changed? Was it they who had caused this war? Was it they who were out for blood of their enemy? No, all his people wanted was freedom and they were trying with all their power to obtain that freedom by retreating to Montana rather than fighting for their homeland. What was going to happen to them? How could he keep them safe, he wondered, now that Howard had more supplies?

After a council with White Bird, Looking Glass, Young Chief and Joseph, Ollikut decided to have Joseph move camp and start for Lolo Pass. The other chiefs and Ollikut, now considered the war chief, would stay with some warriors and stop Howard from following.

The soldiers numbered 560 strong; the warriors counted just over a hundred. The soldiers fought on command. The Indians fought more as small groups and individuals. Howard had positioned his men on the north side of the canyon. They had a cannon and many rifles. Ollikut did not wish to wait for Howard to attack but rather wanted to move in fast with the first light of day.

With 24 men, Ollikut rode Henawit across the canyon floor while the other chiefs took warriors and attacked from the sides and down from the top of the north hill just before Ollikut got within range. Ollikut had held the Army's attention long enough for the others to get into position and fire. Now the forces of Howard's command were surrounded. Knowing he could not win such a battle, Ollikut was satisfied just to keep them pinned down while Joseph guided the people to the pass.

The battle raged all that day. Three warriors had been killed. That night Ollikut and six warriors sneaked into Howard's camp and ran off all the pack mules. The next day the battle continued, but Howard was very concerned over the loss of the mules. He sent a party to find them, but Ollikut intercepted the party and they were all killed. Some warriors drove the mules many miles downstream toward the fort. With this heading, the mules continued the rest of the way on their own.

After 36 hours of fighting and the loss of four warriors, Ollikut collected his warriors and rode for Lolo Pass. Howard was stopped and had no way to follow them. Once the mules arrived at the fort, another supply company was sent out to see what the problem was. This company helped the disheartened Howard back to the fort.

Chapter 17

MORE WAR

The scouts Ollikut had left behind came back to camp and reported Howard had returned to the fort this time. There was much rejoicing in the Indian camp that night. It was all over. They were free at last of Howard and his orders.

They camped at Lolo Hot Springs at the foot of the east slope of the Bitterroot Mountains. They could see the Bitterroot Valley, but were not sure how the white settlers would treat them or if they would have trouble with the unfriendly Flathead Indians. They felt the Crows would give them help if they could reach their camp.

The hot mineral water at the springs felt good after the long, hard ride over Lolo Pass. The trail had been narrow and the edge sometimes dropped off two thousand feet to the canyon floor.

After a two day stay at the hot springs, they decided to move on. What Ollikut didn't know was that Howard had telegraphed ahead to Missoula and ordered Captain Rawn of the Seventh Calvary to intercept the Nez Perce. This he soon learned from his forward scouts as Captain Rawn, with thirty soldiers and two hundred volunteers, rode twelve miles up the Bitterroot Valley to the mouth of Lolo Canyon, then eight miles up the canyon to a narrow area. There they set up a barricade.

Old White Bird knew of a trail higher up the mountain that would bypass the barricade. This is just what they needed. They did not want a head-on battle with the soldiers. Using the upper trail, they passed within sight of the barricade but just out of gun range. Then they dropped down in the canyon behind and below the soldiers and volunteers.

Captain Rawn did not want a running fight for Howard had told him how deceptive these Indians were and how fast their spotted horses were. Ollikut approached the barricade head on. He stopped just out of rifle range.

"Did you come for a fight?" Ollikut hollered.

"We came to stop you from entering the valley and that's what we must do," Captain Rawn yelled back.

"If you look around, you will see that you are surrounded on both sides. If you want war, many of your soldiers will die. We do not want this. We do not want to lose our warriors either."

"I can't let you by. These are my orders."

A leader of the volunteers rode over to Captain Rawn. "You may have orders to stay and fight but, as I remember, these Nez Perce have always been peaceful as they rode through the valley. We're not getting killed for your orders."

Without the volunteers, there was little Captain Rawn could do to stop the Nez Perce.

"I will let you pass if you promise there will be no killing in the valley."

"I can promise we will do no killing in the valley," Ollikut said.

On his return, he telegraphed Howard that the Indians had bypassed their defenses.

The volunteers were happy to retreat without a fight. The Nez Perce had used this trail across the pass to go to buffalo country for as long as any of the pioneers could remember. They had never caused any problems. They were only remembered for their peaceful manner and their fine horses. They generally traded with the settlers as they traveled through the valley. The settlers, however, had heard of the trouble at Lapwai and knew only that it was Nez Perce that had been killing and burning. They were quite apprehensive about dealing with the Indians at first, but then they had never had any trouble before.

Many of the food staples, such as sugar and salt, had been lost in the river crossings or along the trail. They had brought their gold and currency to pay for the things they needed. It was surprising to Ollikut how helpful these people were and how some even said that the soldiers were in the wrong and they hoped the Nez Perce found a place to live again. This was the treatment Ollikut wished they could receive from all the white people.

Once they had obtained all the supplies they needed, they again headed east. They passed through the Bitterroot Valley without incident for even Captain Rawn had returned to the fort at Missoula.

It was now August 6. They had arrived at the Big Hole Camp which was used by Indians going to and coming from the buffalo country. There they met Poker Joe, a half-breed who wanted to join them. He was just returning from hunting buffalo and heard that Chief Rainbow and his band had been captured and sent to prison in Oklahoma. The Oklahoma reservation was where all the hard to handle Indians were sent. It was hot and humid and many died there. Poker Joe did not want to live on the Lapwai reservation and did not want to end up in Oklahoma so he decided to travel with his retreating friends.

That night Wahtitats rode around camp saying he had seen in a vision that he would be killed, and he was ready to die. This was a bad omen.

Even worse was the old medicine man, Halya Lakonnin, who

told his son, Speaking Thunder, "I see the future. It is dark with blood. I do not want to know you are killed. All going will die or see bondage. Return home, my son, or you will surely die."

Speaking Thunder did not return. He was not interested in being put on a reservation or far away in prison. He said, "I would rather die than go back now." His father left the column the next day to return to Lapwai.

These two events upset the people just when they were in Montana and thought they were safe. What did this mean? Were there more wars to be fought? Ollikut was very uneasy and took council with the other chiefs. Looking Glass felt very confident that they were safe and there would be no more soldiers. He said, "We have long ago left Howard and his soldiers. Our scouts have seen no signs of anyone following, even as far as two days back. We can rest in safety for a few days." They all decided that the people needed the rest and the animals could use the time to graze and become stronger.

Ollikut remembered back to his dream on his quest. He had now seen some battles but not all those that the Great Spirit told him in the dream. In his dream, he had seen the spotted horse saving his people in many battles which is what they were doing. In the dream, the Great Spirit never foretold the outcome of these battles. He wondered, would they survive or perish?

Chapter 18
SOLDIERS IN THE INDIAN CAMP

General Howard was not one to be beat on his own game. He was very much in awe with the military maneuvers that he had seen and heard about. In comments to the press concerning the battles he was quoted as saying, "The Wallowa Chief's brilliance and remarkable strategies were something to observe. No general could have chosen a safer position or one that would be more likely to puzzle and obstruct a pursuing foe." The newspaper reporters made it appear as though Joseph was some kind of Indian Napoleon. He was becoming famous all over the nation for his defensive retreats that left the army with their pants down and defeats recorded in the records.

Ollikut had no way of knowing or did he care what was said about the war or who were the chiefs in charge. He was only interested in seeing his people to a safe place.

A telegraph message was sent to Colonel Gibbons by General Howard. "Move immediately to the Big Hole and cut off the escape of the Nez Perce." Howard then moved out to follow the trail and arrive at the Big Hole where he hoped Gibbons would have Joseph pinned down.

Colonel Gibbons was a red-nosed, middle-aged officer who had a mediocre career in the Civil War. He had no experience fighting Indians but presumed he was surely a whole lot smarter than any heathen Indian. Assembling his troops, he prepared for a forced march to the Big Hole.

On the eve of August 8, three Indians arrived at the camp from the north and called at the tepee of Ollikut. They were two treaty

Nez Perce, Grizzly Bear Boy, his brother Horn Hide Dresser, and a Yakima by the name of Owhi. The three had served as scouts for Colonel Nelson Miles in the Sioux country of the Yellowstone. They had heard about the Nez Perce wars and, disdaining Miles, had made their way to the Flathead reservation. There they had met the Nez Perce, Eagle From the Light, who even before the outbreak of the war had become disgusted with conditions in Idaho and settled down with some Flathead friends. At the suggestion of Eagle From the Light, they had come south to meet the warring bands and propose to them that they head north, pass through the Flathead reservation and cross into Canada only a short distance away where they could find safety.

A council was held. Looking Glass did not like the plan to head north through Flathead country. He was afraid they would end up fighting the Flathead too. Food would be in much shorter supply than by going east and then north through Crow country. White Bird wanted to get to the Grand Mother's Land as fast as they could, but Looking Glass was more persuasive. They agreed to go east and then north to Canada.

Gibbons had been traveling for five days with 146 enlisted men and 17 officers. He stopped at Missoula and sent word to Howard that he was pursuing the Nez Perce at once and would hold them down until Howard arrived.

On the morning of August 9, Colonel Gibbons and his men fought through underbrush and marshes for five miles, then waded the Big Hole River and were in a position from which the Indians did not expect any attack. In fact, they were not even thinking of being attacked when the soldiers came storming into camp with guns blazing. Captain Logan shot and killed Young Chief before he could get his rifle. His wife picked up the rifle and shot Logan through the head. Within twenty minutes the soldiers had driven the Indians from their camp. They had left without their belongings and, in many cases, without their guns and ammunition. Gibbons had ordered the men to shoot anything that moved and that's just what they did. Women and children were killed, some still in their bedrolls. A daughter of Chief Looking Glass and Joseph's sick wife were killed.

White Bird started a brush fire between themselves and the soldiers to burn the soldiers out. It burned only a short distance when a wind came up and stopped its progress. This was strong medicine.

Ollikut could hardly believe his eyes when he saw the soldiers. He had jumped up and shot two soldiers at the front of his tepee. Seeing there was no place to fight from there, he grabbed his son and Wetatonmi and ran for the cover of the trees. Once there, he collected all the fighting men he could find and tried to form a plan. By then the soldiers had set fire to most of the camp. Some tepees were in flames. Ollikut knew they had lost a lot of people in that first attack, and he was not interested in losing any more than he had to. Many were for retreating and leaving everything. Ollikut said, "Why should we retreat? Since the world was made, brave men have fought for their women and children. Now fight!"

With the Indians in the timber and the soldiers on the flat, there was a real advantage for sharp shooters. Soldiers began to fall over one after another. Fear struck in the hearts of the soldiers for they had the river to their back and the woods full of Indians in front of them. Gibbons finally gained control of his troops and moved them back to an area where he told them to dig trenches to fight from.

Captain Caltin, one of the last to reach the position, saw the thick stand of trees around them that was an excellent hiding place for Indian snipers and exclaimed, "Who the hell called a halt here?"

When he was told that Gibbons had ordered it, he snapped, "I don't give a damn. It's a hell of a place to make a stand."

The Indians took advantage of the trees around the trenched soldiers and began shooting. The soldiers were now pinned down. Wahchumyus was killed by a soldier's bullet. This made his war brother, Pahkatos, very sad. Pahkatos and Wahchumyus' fathers were war brothers and had been killed in the same battle many years before. The two sons had vowed they, too, would die in the same battle. After sitting by Wahchymyus for a few minutes, Pahkatos jumped up and ran down the hill firing at the soldiers. He dropped two before a volley of shots hit him, killing him on the spot.

A captured soldier was brought to Ollikut. One of the warriors raised his gun, but Ollikut said not to shoot him like this.

"Look down there at the women and children you have killed," Poker Joe ordered. Just then another warrior fired a shot through the soldiers head.

What are we coming to, thought Ollikut. Is there no mercy on either side? Just kill, kill, kill! Then he remembered that is what the spirit in his dream had shown him, many battles and many dead.

Cut off and without prospect of early relief, the soldiers' position worsened rapidly. They were running out of water and food. Their ammunition was low because they had been separated from their mules loaded with supplies which had since been collected by the warriors.

That night was tough on the soldiers; they had no food, water or blankets. It was a cold night and many were wounded. They had one horse that had just been shot and they butchered him and ate what they could, but some got sick from the poorly cooked raw meat.

Ollikut had sent word for Joseph to go back to camp to get everything they could use, also to take the pack mules with the

172

soldiers' food, ammunition and blankets with them. He and his men would hold the soldiers here while they made their escape.

Joseph counted 59 dead Indians. Many more were wounded. His heart was very heavy for his dead wife. He still had his daughter, Running Spring. She was now with Wetatonmi and Young Ollikut.

There were 31 dead soldiers and many lay wounded. Joseph thought of attending to them, but he knew they must leave that sad place as fast as possible.

The soldiers remained pinned down all night long. A scout finally brought Ollikut word that more soldiers were within a half-day's ride. Ollikut decided to give them a few more volleys of fire and then follow the trail that Joseph had taken. This he did, killing a few more soldiers.

Overtaking Joseph, Ollikut was told just how bad it had been. In all 89 Indians had either been killed at the battle site or had died during the night, but only twelve of these were warriors. The rest were women and children. The people felt anger towards Looking Glass for giving them a false sense of security while at the Big Hole River camp.

The Montana white settlers now turned against them, as had the settlers in Idaho. Many volunteers had been killed in the battles and their families mourned. Ollikut knew his people were not safe. They knew their enemy would kill not only their brave men but their women and children. Emotions were torn.

Joseph had been propelled by fate through this, almost against his will. He was against killing on moral grounds and that was why he had accepted the role of guard for the women and children. Now he knew that role would be hard to maintain with all the whites trying to kill them. He may have to kill to save his people.

There were many times during the retreat, thought Ollikut, when we could have made war on white women and children, but we did not. We would feel ashamed to do so. Joseph, he knew, was ashamed to kill anyone, and the prospect of a future in which their people would have to kill to stay alive haunted him. Joseph was almost like a ghost since the Big Hole battle. After losing his wife and baby, he was very withdrawn.

For every soldier they had killed, ten more would come back in his place, Ollikut knew. But no one took the place of a dead warrior. They had lost many warriors, others had left on their own, thus they were getting fewer in numbers of fighting men. They had lost many spotted horses and all the cattle some time ago.

"We can't stay here any longer," Ollikut told Joseph.

"If we try to travel, we will lose more," Joseph responded.

"If we don't, we will all be killed right here. Looking Glass, what do you advise?"

"I think if we get to the Crow nation, they will help us fight the soldiers," Looking Glass said.

"I'm not sure the Crows will help us," White Bird said. "They have never been friendly to my people."

"We must do something," Ollikut advised.

Just then a Sioux brave rode into camp.

"Where is Chief Joseph?"

"I'm right here."

"I bring you bad news. After Chief Crazy Horse killed yellow hair, the Army brought many more soldiers and have captured or run Crazy Horse's people into hiding."

"We must try to reach the Crow and hope they will help us," Looking Glass said.

There were a few minutes of silence; then they all agreed.

Chapter 19

AND MORE WAR

Howard arrived shortly after Ollikut and his warriors had left the Big Hole. He found a pitiful sight of cold and crying soldiers, many badly wounded. Others were completely unstable. The doctors helped with the wounded, and they were all fed and made comfortable. This slowed Howard almost a day and a half.

Howard's Bannock scouts led by Buffalo Horn spent the time digging up the graves and scalping the dead Indians and mutilating their bodies. This upset the Christian Howard but he did nothing to stop it.

The remainder of the Nez Perce band under Joseph's leadership had moved on toward Yellowstone Park. Many were wounded badly. Two died the first day and were buried. It was a custom for those too sick to go on to stay behind so they would not hold up the rest of the party and jeopardize their lives. At the first night's camp after the battle, eleven were left in camp when they moved on. Within a day Howard's scouts and forward guard had reached their camp and as the soldiers stood by, the Bannock scouts cruelly murdered and scalped the sick Nez Perce while screaming and dancing in a wild frenzy.

Ollikut and his warriors held back to see what the Army was going to do. Once Ollikut and his men reached Joseph and his group of distraught Indians, another council was held. It was again agreed upon to continue on towards Crow Country. White Bird still argued for a turn north to go straight to Canada where Sitting Bull's people were now in exile. Looking Glass felt sure the Crows would help them and hide them until they could move on.

Poker Joe was to guide the party through Yellowstone Park because he had just come through it only a few weeks before. He guided them south through the Salmon River Valley and on to Camas Meadows. On August 20 they stopped in the meadows for a needed rest.

Young Ollikut was holding up very well, considering he was only six years old. He had ridden a horse and helped drive the horses all day long. Wetatonmi was busy tending the wounded and all the while wondering if Ollikut would be next to fall. Death was all around her. She was not so afraid for herself as she was sick at heart over the happenings of the past month and the feelings of hopelessness for the future. If only there was a way for the children to be saved, she thought, but she knew they would not be spared by the soldiers. This bothered her more than anything. How could these men who called themselves Christians murder women and children? Ollikut and his warriors had not when they had the chance. Why, why, oh why did these white soldiers have no honor, she wondered.

While traveling through the Salmon River country Ollikut had directed his men to collect all the settler's horses so Howard would have no fresh mounts to come after them with. This cost the lives of five white settlers who fought for their horses. Some did not fight and were not hurt. A wagon with three men and two women was captured. Ollikut told them they were prisoners but would not be hurt if they did not try to escape. He asked them to help guide his people to the entrance of the Great Park of Shooting Waters. This was agreed, but when night came the men tried to escape. Two were killed and the other wounded. The next day the women and the wounded man, who later died, were set free. They were of no use to the party now.

Their uncertainty about these trails made the Nez Perce linger at Camas Meadows. Poker Joe was not sure which would be the fastest or the easiest route to take into and through the park. He had only been around the south side of the lake, but he knew there was a trail north of the lake that would go east, then turn north towards Billings,

Montana.

Howard wasted no time in closing in on the Nez Perce. His Bannock scouts soon brought back word that the Nez Perce were camped in the Camas Meadows only fifteen miles ahead. Howard was sure he had them this time. Just in case they did slip away, he dispatched forty men to Targhee Pass to stop the party if he was unsuccessful. That night Howard camped at the edge of the big grassy meadow which spread for about ten miles. The Nez Perce were camped on the edge of the meadow about five miles ahead. Howard planned an early morning attack just like Gibbons had used. He would ride through the camp with his 400 men and that would be the end of the fight.

The Nez Perce scouts brought back word to Ollikut that the troops were within five miles and camped for the night. Ollikut new the people were tired. He could not move them tonight. He must find a way to stop Howard's attack.

The night before, Black Hair, though wounded badly from two shots, had a strong vision in which he had seen the warriors going back over the trail to the Army camp and coming away with the soldier's horses. Black Hair's son, Yellow Elk, brought this information to the council that evening and it was decided that this should be done.

The raiding party led by Ollikut and Looking Glass waited until a little after midnight to start. Within another hour they were too close to ride, so half the group under Looking Glass went on foot to the edge of the camp. They were able to get past the first guard, and once at the tethered horses, they began to cut them loose. Suddenly a guard said, "Who goes there?" An Indian named Going Out, fired his rifle killing the guard. This awoke the whole camp. Ollikut had to attack them to save Looking Glass and his party. Looking Glass and his men continued cutting horses and mules loose as Ollikut and his warriors came down on the camp whooping and hollering. They were waving their blanket coats and firing at the waking soldiers. The

177

soldiers were in panic. They could not find their pants and boots, let alone their rifles. Hardly a shot was fired by the soldiers as Ollikut and his men rode straight through the camp. Now many of the soldiers had their rifles in hand, but the loose horses racing towards them sent them in panic again. The Indians and their stolen horses were through camp and running hard away to the east before Howard's soldiers could regroup for a fight.

As they raced out, Ollikut realized that they had only taken about half the General's stock. He could see more horses picketed in another area. He had gotten only the pack stock and the volunteer's horses, but that was enough to slow the troops for a while.

Howard stayed another day at his camp even though Buffalo Horn and the Bannock scouts wanted to pursue the Nez Perce right then. Loading all their supplies on the saddle horses, they continued following the Nez Perce. Howard was sure his detachment, under Lieutenant Bacon, would stop the Indians at Targhee Pass.

Luckily for Ollikut and his people, Bacon had not arrived at the Pass by the time they crossed over into the Yellowstone country. The road ahead was downhill and the game plentiful. There were fish in the streams so thick they could be speared.

The scouts reported to Ollikut that Howard had reached the Pass about a day behind them and had turned around and gone back. Had they finally made it to safety, Ollikut wondered?

Low on horses and ammunition and short of food, Howard realized he could not follow the Nez Perce on their strong spotted horses any longer. His men were tired and cold. They had only their summer uniforms on and up in the high country it was now getting quite cold at night. September was only a few days away and snow would soon be on the way. With this in mind Howard departed for Virginia City which was north of their position to resupply and send a message to his superiors.

Chapter 20

CAPTURE ASSURED

Further advice from General Sherman, Howard's Commanding Officer, assured Howard that despite his ineffective maneuvers, adequate steps were being taken by troops of the Department of Dakota to trap the Nez Perce in the park. On the north were two companies of the Second and Seventh Cavalries. Their job was to block the park exit at Mammoth Hot Springs. On the east, Colonel Samuel D. Sturgis with six companies of the Seventh Cavalry, 360 troops strong, were waiting for the Nez Perce. They were to guard the Clark Fork River route. Major Hart, with five companies of the Fifth Cavalry and one hundred scouts, were to watch the Shoshone River exit near Cody. Another of the Fifth Cavalry's Colonels, Wesley Merritt, with ten companies was on the Wind River to the south. Colonel Miles at Fort Keogh near Miles City was ready for a forced march to whatever point at which the Nez Perce were intercepted. With Howard again dogging them from the west, they were virtually surrounded.

The Yellowstone Park had been established by Congress in 1872 and over the past five years many visitors had come to see the marvelous sights. This year had been no exception. Few, if any, visitors knew of the war that was taking place around them.

The first vacationer the Nez Perce came across was an old prospector, John Shively, who knew the country between them and the Crows' homeland. They obtained his services as a guide and continued. Shively stayed on as the guide for a week and then left for his home in northern Montana.

There were other encounters with park visitors, some of which ended in the death of the men in the party, but no women were harmed. Joseph and Ollikut saw to that. One captured woman was held at Joseph's campfire for the night for her own protection. She tried unsuccessfully to engage Joseph in conversation. She found the Chief somber and silent, but she reported later that, "The noble redman we read of was more nearly embodied in this Indian than in any I have ever met. Grave and dignified, he looked like a chief. His brother Ollikut, however, appeared to be in charge of all the warriors. Joseph spent most of his time in camp helping the older people and conducting the camp activity."

By September 1, Howard had closed in again from the west. He had forces in place on every side of the Park. The War Department, consequently, issued news releases to the effect that the Indians were virtually captured. The army had its best Indian fighters leading the attack against the tired and tattered Indians. It was certain, in Howard's mind, that there could be no escape for them this time.

Sturgis and his cavalry were waiting for the Nez Perce on the Clark Fork River. This man was advanced in years. He had lost a son at the Little Big Horn when Custer, Sitting Bull and Crazy Horse fought. Sturgis had been given Custer's old unit's name and guidon. He and his troops were anxious to vindicate the Seventh Calvary's honor. It mattered not that these were not Sioux Indians or that they had women and children with them. They were Indians.

After waiting for sometime Sturgis grew impatient. His

scouts reported Clark Fork Canyon virtually impassable because of fallen trees and rock slides. Sturgis was concerned that the Nez Perce had taken another route and he would not get a crack at them.

The trip was showing its wear on the Nez Perce. They were tired and some were wounded. Yet, they had used the stolen horses to pack their supplies and had saved their spotted horses for riding. The rest were driven along, grazing at nights on the lush grass in the Park.

Knowing his party could not win a battle, Ollikut kept pushing on. He had scouts out in every direction. He had learned that the enemy could come out of anywhere. He was going to know as much as he could as early as he could. Scouts returned with news of Sturgis and of his scouts looking for their location. Ollikut knew he could not fight past Sturgis so he must be able to outmaneuver him. If he started along the Shoshone River, Sturgis would surely learn of it and try to cut him off. Once Sturgis moved east to the Shoshone, Ollikut planned to take his people back to Clark's Fork and be out of the Park heading for Crow country.

His plan worked. Sturgis took the bait and rushed full speed to cut the Nez Perce off on the Shoshone. Once he made his move, Ollikut had riders ride out a mile in all directions then circle back to a trail leading to Clark's Fork.

After waiting a half day on the Shoshone, Sturgis began pushing toward where the Indians should be. By the end of the day he had reached the point where the Indians had made their disappearing act. He could see that Howard had even been there before him and was now on the tracks of the Nez Perce ahead of him.

Sturgis knew he had blundered. Howard would think that he was ahead of the Nez Perce and would stop them at Clark's Fork Pass. Now the Indians would have no one ahead of them and only Howard trailing behind.

The going was rough through the canyon but they made it, thanks to their tough spotted horses. Ollikut was a hero. They had outsmarted the Army again. The people were very happy. They felt sure they could make it now. They were still a day ahead of Howard and Crow country was just ahead.

Looking Glass went ahead to talk to the Crow chief and ask permission to cross their land. He found the chief friendly but also found that the River Bottom Crow were now allied with the Army. In fact, some of the chief's braves had gone to scout for the Army and were to meet Sturgis and Howard to scout for them. It was impossible for his people to help the Nez Perce.

"The Nez Perce people are doomed." The Crow chief told Looking Glass, "Surrender before you are all killed."

With this information, Looking Glass rode back to the band of Nez Perce feeling very dejected and sad. What could he tell his people? It was he who had told them that the Crow Indians would help. They possibly should have turned north at the Big Hole and ridden straight for the Grand Mother Country and Sitting Bull.

At Looking Glass's return, Ollikut called a council to discuss this new information. There were sad hearts in the council. Some were very bitter towards Looking Glass. Especially upset was White Bird who had counseled to go north at the Big Hole Camp.

Meanwhile, Howard had found out Sturgis was behind him so he waited for his junior officer to catch up with much displeasure. Together they planned the next strategy. A message was sent to Colonel Miles at Fort Keogh on the Missouri River. He was to move northwest and intercept the Nez Perce before they reached Canada. Howard didn't want the Nez Perce to get close to Canada. He sent Sturgis on ahead as soon as possible to watch the Nez Perce while he came up slower with the cannons and supplies.

With a minimum of supply animals to slow him down, Sturgis closed in fast on the Nez Perce column. By September 12 they were in sight of the Indians.

During the council, after Looking Glass returned, it was decided to travel through Crow country even without their permission and protection. If they could reach the Mountain Crow bands, Looking Glass felt sure they could get help. Two years before, he and his band of warriors had helped these Indians defeat the Blackfeet and they owed him a debt.

As the Nez Perce crossed the Yellowstone River, the scouts brought word of the sighting of Sturgis and his cavalry a few miles back. In the distance they could see a narrow canyon reaching up to the top of a small mountain range. It was Canyon Creek. Ollikut encouraged them all to ride as hard as they could for that canyon. It would give them less area to defend; and if they made it before Sturgis could get around them, they would possibly leave him again.

Their fast spotted horses were too much for Sturgis. As they both dashed for the canyon in a running battle, it was Ollikut and his band that arrived at the mouth of the canyon first. Sturgis could see he had been beaten, yet he sent a company of cavalry to climb the hills on each side of the canyon.

The warriors stopped at the mouth of the canyon while

the women and children, still led by Joseph, continued up the canyon. Ollikut and the warriors tried to stall the troops while Joseph got their people to the top of the canyon.

The Great Spirit must be guiding our bullets, Ollikut thought, as he saw the warriors pick off one after another of the troopers trying to climb the hills. Soon they were in complete confusion and retreat.

Sturgis, in the meantime, had sent two companies on foot through tall sagebrush to attack the warriors at the mouth of the draw. This was a mistake because Ollikut and his men could see down on them and they didn't have a chance. The battle raged for half a day. Sturgis was stopped and was losing heavily. The troopers were now shooting from a distance because there was no cover closer up.

One by one Ollikut sent his men off to catch up with their families. At last only one old Indian was left. He was such a good shot, however, that he kept Sturgis' whole command pinned down until dark and then he melted into the night. Sturgis had once more been out maneuvered and his men outshot.

The battle had not been a complete victory for the Nez Perce. They had lost over 400 more spotted horses in the race for the canyon, three Indians had been killed and two more wounded. The soldiers lost over 25 men in the attack with many more wounded.

Chapter 21

THE RACE GOES ON

Although Sturgis was stopped for the time, he wasn't defeated. He sent back to Howard for scouts. By the next morning, they were in camp. He instructed the Bannock and Crow scouts, which totaled over 200, to attack and harass the Nez Perce until he could catch up with fresh soldiers.

The next few days were a nightmare for the Nez Perce families. The Bannocks and Crows had caught up with them and were attacking time and time again. Ollikut kept the people moving while the Bannocks and Crows got only a few horses, most of which had been stolen from the army. Ollikut thought this would quench their desire more than blood. After a day of fighting, the Crows drove off over 500 horses and departed for their people. The Bannocks had nowhere to go with the horses so they kept on fighting. No one could leave the protection of the camp in safety. Some tried and paid for it with their lives. The Nez Perce warriors protected their families with their lives in a way never surpassed. Ollikut and Joseph were proud to be Nez Perce and to live and fight with such brave men, women and children. Many times the women and older children also had to shoot and kill to save their own lives.

The Nez Perce slipped out at dawn the next day. They soon arrived at the Musselshell River and crossed ahead of the Bannocks. Ollikut left a group of warriors at the crossing to stop the Bannocks. This was not an easy job for the Bannocks had a taste of blood and wanted to kill. They paid a bloody price trying to cross the river and finally gave up and went back to where Howard and Sturgis had again united.

There was no more hope left in the hearts of Joseph's people for a home in the Buffalo Country. Not even their cousins, the Crows, would help them. They knew now that they must travel straight for the Grand Mother Land. White Bird had told them that in Grand Mother's Land they would have equal justice as the Red Coats did not fire first. They would be protected from Howard and his men, and Sitting Bull's people would be happy to see them. This sounded good, but the few people still remaining were sad at heart and tired of the long trail. Each time they thought the fighting was over, it would come again from another direction. What did the Great Spirit expect of them? Were they not good, honest people who had harmed no one while they were in the Wallowa? What was to happen? Would there be no safety? Yet, every soul knew they must press on. It was too late now to stop. There had been no prisoners taken by the soldiers yet. Ollikut and Joseph had let many wounded soldiers go after taking their guns and horses.

Ollikut's heart was heavy. He was concerned for Wetatonmi and Young Ollikut. They had come this far safely, but what about tomorrow? Each day a few more died. When would it end? Every precaution had been taken for their safety. Joseph had personally watched over them as well as his own daughter who was with them. Ollikut had been able to spend little time with them the past two months. Most of the time he had been fighting or preparing for a fight. If only the fighting was to result in their getting safely into Canada, Ollikut thought it still wouldn't justify their plight. If not, then what had it been for? So many had died. Every family, save his own, had lost a member. The graves of these loved ones lay far behind them. Many did not even find a grave but lay where they fell. The sick and elderly were giving up in increasing numbers, staying behind in camp or dropping out of the column during the day to find a place where they could die alone, a place where the Bannocks might not find their bodies.

The horses, too, were getting sore backs and becoming lame. Some would stray at night, and others had to be abandoned on the trail. The spotted horse had shown his stamina to all the soldiers. They were the talk of the Eastern horse fancier. It had always been thought that the Indian pony was of inferior quality, but the Nez Perce's spotted horses were a match for any horse. The soldiers knew it well.

Knowing the soldiers would not wait long before coming after them,

Ollikut advised his people they must move fast to get to Canada. The next 36 hours they covered 78 miles. This was proof to Ollikut and the world that the Nez Perce people and spotted horses had heart. By September 23 they had reached Crow Island, a supply point on the Missouri River for points north, west and southwest. A boat brought goods up to this point for the trappers and ranchers in Montana.

By luck a boat had just unloaded a cargo of supplies. The scouts reported a small detachment of soldiers and some civilians at the landing. Ollikut knew he could overrun the whites and take what they needed, but he did not want to lose another man, woman or child. Instead, he and Poker Joe went under a truce flag to talk to the whites and try to buy the food their people so desperately needed. They had killed a few buffalo three days ago, but that was gone and there was no fresh meat.

The owner of the dock said that the supplies were not his to sell. Ollikut told him he could take them if he wanted, but he would rather buy them. The owner offered them only a side of pork and some beans. They took the food and went back to their camp. This was not enough food to give everyone a taste, let alone to fill their bellies.

Ollikut collected some warriors and attacked the whites. They drove them back to a hill some yards away. While the whites were held down under fire, other Indians took what they needed from the dock and set fire to the rest.

No one was killed and only one white had been wounded in the fighting. That night there was food for all, new army blankets, some guns and ammunition. This cargo had been sent up river at Howard's request for his resupply. Ollikut had taken good care of the army's supplies.

Again Ollikut pushed the people on towards Bear Paw and then to Canada. Bear Paw was a place with many buffalo chips for fires that would warm them before going on to Canada. It was halfway between where they were and Canada. They were getting close now. They could tell by the sight of the mountains in the far distance and their snowy mountain tops. Each day it seemed the snow got closer down the mountains. It had already snowed on them a half dozen times in the past three weeks. The nights were getting cold and the new blankets felt good. So much of their supplies had been lost or stolen that the new supplies came just in time.

That evening Looking Glass called a council. He said, "Our people are tired. You have driven them too hard, Ollikut. We are ahead of Howard and we can stop earlier and travel slower so the warriors can hunt and keep fresh meat in our bellies."

"I have been trying to keep our people from being killed. My wife and son are as tired as your family, but they want to get safely to Canada. I leave it up to the council if they wish you or me to lead them now," Ollikut said in disgust.

Those of the council were tired of the fast pace, too. They had some wounded that would surely die if they kept up this pace. They decided Looking Glass was right.

"If this is what you wish, so be it. Just remember my words. If we slow down, the soldiers will surely catch us and we will all be killed." With this, Ollikut left the council. He was very sad. He had tried so hard to do the right thing. Now, even Joseph had agreed that they should slow down.

As he reached his camp, he had great fears of what was to come. He told Wetatonmi of these fears. She knew he had done all he could to guide them through the soldiers and on to Canada. She was very sad about the decision that was made at the council, both for Ollikut and for herself and Young Ollikut's safety. After enduring so much, she knew it was no time to slow down and relax. Could the chiefs not see what had happened the times before and that it would happen again?

They talked that night of leaving the band and making their way north as fast as possible, but Ollikut knew the Assiniboines Indians were a very cruel and unfriendly tribe. He did not wish his family to be caught by them to be tortured and killed. They agreed it was better to stay together with the rest of the Nez Perce than try to hurry them along.

It took three days for them to get to Bear Paw, a distance of about 50 miles. These were easy days with only a few Cheyenne Indians seen on the horizon. The people began to believe Looking Glass and became slow to start in the mornings, then stopped early in the afternoon.

Chapter 2 2

BEAR PAW

At Bear Paw fires were built of buffalo chips and kept going day and night because of the cold. The first night it snowed three inches. Everyone was shivering with cold because of the north wind that followed the storm. The buffalo chips were wet and hard to get to burn. Nevertheless the women and children kept the fires going as best they could.

Buffalo had been seen in the distance the day before. The families were running short of fresh meat again so Looking Glass counseled to rest a few days at Bear Paw before continuing to Canada. They could see Canada from Bear Paw. It was only an easy two-day ride away. They could surely outrun the troops if they did come. They would have a day's notice from their scouts if Howard started to close in. Their fast horses could easily outrun the poorer army horses he advised.

Looking Glass had sent a runner to Sitting Bull over a month ago telling him that they needed help. He asked Sitting Bull to bring fresh horses and warriors. Looking Glass was sure help was on its way. He even sent out two scouts to find him and tell him where they were.

The only thing Looking Glass didn't know was that Crazy Horse's Oglala Sioux had surrendered and were in a stockade camp further east. Crazy Horse himself had been killed by the soldiers while walking from the guard house to his trial.

The people had three days of slow travel and felt more rested than they had for days. It was time to move north, Ollikut counseled. "We have rested and eaten well. We have warm blankets; let us now move on before we have cold bodies." No one would listen.

The scouts had reported that Howard still wasn't close. They felt safe and wanted more rest before the cold ride to Canada.

Miles was coming up fast. His Cheyenne scouts had reported sighting the Nez Perce and knew right where they were. They did not get too close because they didn't want the Nez Perce to start running again. With this news, Miles took an advanced column of soldiers ahead to pin them down while the remainder of his command came up later with supplies and additional troops.

The Nez Perce children were playing in the warm afternoon sun in the draws and coulees along the river. The snow had melted and the ground was drying. It seemed so good to all the people just to rest and watch the children play and to see the sick feeling better. The hunters had brought in fresh buffalo meat and all their bellies were full. The people felt sure they would make it now. They were finally going to be safe and free.

This feeling was not with Ollikut. He had a strange feeling of being trapped. All he could think of was leaving this place. That night Yellow Wolf came to Ollikut and Joseph and asked if they wished to go with him north. He and 63 other people were ready to leave. They had no wish to wait any longer. He, too, was concerned that the soldiers would soon find them. Ollikut pleaded with Joseph to go then and leave Looking Glass and the rest to go when they pleased. Joseph would not be swayed. He was not leaving the rest of the people. "There is strength in numbers," he said. He also felt that there was adequate time to get to Canada before the soldiers could close in.

What more could Ollikut do? He didn't want to leave his people either, yet he didn't want to risk his family's lives for the rest's stupidity. Finally he told Yellow Wolf to go without him, but Ollikut asked him to tell Sitting Bull of their situation and ask him to send warriors to meet them and give them protection to Canada. Yellow Wolf agreed and departed quickly for the north. Neither Ollikut nor Yellow Wolf realized how far away Sitting Bull's camp was.

That night Ollikut, Wetatonmi and Young Ollikut talked of times of the past years when they rode to Spokane House so Young Ollikut might see the great cities and the white man's developments. They had so much joy and fullness of life then. Ollikut had many horses and cattle, and through his wise trading had much gold set away for their use. He told Wetatonmi that the Great Spirit had been very good to them to have given them such a beautiful place to live and given him such a special wife and son. Why is it that he had not helped them now when they needed his Spirit most of all? They had lived well and killed no one, so what justice was this that they had received?

Wetatonmi comforted him in thought. She had no answers for his questions. She only knew she had been very happy in the Wallowa with him, and that Young Ollikut was his most precious gift to her. She loved them both very dearly and would give her life for either of them if she were asked.

She told Ollikut that the Great Spirit had been protecting them. Not one of the three had been wounded even though Ollikut had five holes in his clothes where bullets had passed through without more than scratching him. Wetatonmi had been out of danger in almost every battle thanks to Joseph's fast thinking. Ollikut realized too that Joseph had done a marvelous job keeping the women and children as safe as possible while moving the horse herd with them.

The three of them sat talking late into the night. This was one of the few chances they had to be together for many weeks. Young Ollikut asked his father about the battles, but Ollikut said, "We shall talk of good things to be, not bad things that are past." Soon Young Ollikut fell asleep in his father's lap. Ollikut loved his son as his father had loved him. His heart filled with hopes and dreams for this young boy that was so much the image of his father. Soon sleep came over Ollikut and Wetatonmi as they lay in each other's arms.

Waking the next morning, they found their camp very cold. It had snowed a little during the night. The sky was overcast and threatening a big storm. Their fire was soon warm. Ollikut left Wetatonmi with a caress, then bent down and took a long look at Young Ollikut. Wetatonmi felt something inside that she could not explain, but knew she didn't like.

Scouts had been out early and had not yet returned. Ollikut picked up more buffalo chips to keep the fire going, then met with Looking Glass to try to convince him that they must leave today. Looking Glass disagreed saying, "Let's wait one more day and if Sitting Bull has not arrived, we will go north." This was not the answer Ollikut had hoped for, but he couldn't change Looking Glass' mind. The older chief was so sure Sitting Bull would come.

Before breakfast, two scouts arrived from the south with word that Howard was still days away. Ollikut still felt concerned and uneasy. He sent out scouts to the east and west. They could see clearly to the north which had given Looking Glass more support for his argument that they could outrun any soldiers

192

that did attack.

Soon a scout came riding back and reported he had seen stampeding buffalo which was usually a sign of Indians hunting or soldiers, and it was not likely that there were Indians hunting now. Ollikut told everyone to hurry and pack for a long, hard ride. Some started to pack even though they hadn't finished breakfast.

Looking Glass jumped on a horse and rode around camp calling out, "Do not hurry. There is plenty of time; let the children finish eating." Many followed Looking Glass' direction and fed the children, then slowly started packing while the children ran off to play along the stream.

Less than an hour had passed when a scout on the southeastern horizon was seen waving a blanket frantically. Ollikut knew the soldiers were too close. Before the warriors could be collected, two companies of cavalry rode hard for the horse herd. Many of the horses were packed with the supplies and blankets. Others were being held for mounts. The soldiers, shooting and hollering, caused so much panic that the horses stampeded. Joseph and Running Spring were among them getting ready to mount and ride off when the horses stampeded. They were lucky enough to lead their horses into a ravine as the horse herd passed.

Wetatonmi had five horses down in the ravine close to her camp waiting for them. Some of the others had done the same. The soldiers were very successful and got away with over ninety percent of the herd.

Running to the top of the ravine, Ollikut started firing at the soldiers as they passed. One, then another and another were shot off their horses. The soldiers were in plain sight and the sharp-shooting warriors gave them no quarter.

Miles knew if he once had the spotted horses, he had the Nez Perce. That wasn't enough, however. He next sent a full charge of four companies through what was left of the camp. This drove the women and children back up the creek to hide in the ravines and washes. Many were shot while running. The soldiers were in plain sight, and now the warriors with their weapons were in every wash shooting with deadly aim. Soldiers were falling all around. This second assault had cost the army 53 dead in one group. One company lost sixty percent of its men. It was leaderless down to a single sergeant. The bugler blew retreat and the soldiers withdrew to the main line.

It had been just as hard on the Nez Perce because they had lost their only means of escape. They had also lost 22 women and children and eight fighting men.

Miles knew he must make the kill while the Indians were still unorganized so he sent in the Fifth Cavalry to sweep the ridges and get the warriors pushed down to the low ground. The cavalry came at full speed toward the main hollow where they were to ascend to the plateau. The Indians' fire was heavy and yet the soldiers kept coming. With rifles in hand, every cavalryman was firing as fast as he could while riding.

Ollikut lay at the top of the ravine in which he had camped. Wetatonmi and Young Ollikut were hiding under an overhang in the hill. They had staked the horses, but three of them had already broken away. Only Henawit and Wetatonmi's horse were left.

Ollikut knew there was no chance of them making a run for it for the Cheyenne scouts had closed in to the north and were back shooting everything that moved. They were no better than the Bannocks.

If only he could protect his family until the fighting was over, possibly they would be taken prisoners and not treated too harshly. He still feared for their lives because of the blood-thirsty Cheyenne. He had already brought down four soldiers and three Cheyenne. The killing will end at this place, he thought. We will fight no more for there are too many whites and nowhere for us to run, he thought.

His thoughts drifted back to the days at the Wallowa, but he was quickly brought back to reality as a handful of Cheyenne came riding down the river from the north. Turning, he fired three times in succession dropping three riders. They were coming too fast and there were too many of them. He saw one shoot his rifle just as he fell. Ollikut could feel the burning fire go through his chest. The Cheyenne jumped off their horses to scalp him. He knew he could not get them all, but he pulled his rifle in place once more and fired dropping another. Just then Wetatonmi stepped out of her hiding place and shot the remaining two Cheyenne before they could turn around. Ollikut tried to walk towards her but fell and rolled to the bottom of the draw. She and Young Ollikut ran to his side. Looking up, he could still see enough to make her out. The sounds of the war had almost disappeared from his head. All he could think of was his family and the Wallowa. He could see the three of them riding together among the new colts admiring Henawit's fine young sons and daughters. Wetatonmi was smiling with the pride of a Nez Perce princess. She looked more beautiful than Ollikut had ever seen her. Her long black hair was glistening in the sun. Young Ollikut was laughing as he watched the colts playing by their mothers. His thoughts took him back further to when Henawit was just a colt playing by his mother. What dreams he had for the two of them. Why was it all to end here in a cold, damp riverbank over one thousand miles from the Wallowa he loved?

He could feel the life flowing from his body as he reached up to caress Wetatonmi's face. He could not hold up his hand. It slid down to his side. Young Ollikut grabbed it and squeezed it tightly. Ollikut could not see him, but knew that within that small hand would live his blood on through the years. With this thought, Ollikut fell asleep to wake soon in the land beyond the sunrise with the Great Spirit. There he would wait for his family.

Chapter 23
WHAT PRICE IS FREEDOM?

Heartbroken but fearful for her son's life, Wetatonmi once again took refuge in the hill dugout. Soon the shooting stopped.

General Howard had arrived with his troops and cannons. This was the first time he had been able to catch up with the Nez Perce. It was the first time during this war he had really been in battle with them. Realizing he had them pinned down and night was almost on them, he decided to wait for the next day to try his hand at defeating the Nez Perce.

That night was cold and wet. It snowed five inches and most of the Indians were without blankets and no fires were lit. The best they could do was dig deep into the ground and two or three get in a hole and cover it with whatever they could find. Joseph took Wetatonmi and her son in with his daughter. They built a dugout to make it through the night. Young Ollikut was very cold, but he never let a tear fall from his eyes. He and his mother both cried inside all through that night for their beloved Ollikut. Joseph tried to comfort them. He told Wetatonmi, "You know misfortunes will befall the wisest and best people. Death will come to all of us and some out of season. What is past cannot be prevented. Misfortunes grow all around you. Take joy in the life of your son and live now for him as you did for Ollikut before him."

Morning came with an explosion as General Howard had his cannons in place and was firing at the Indian camp. The first shots were high and over the camp. Soon the cannons were set with their tails dug in the ground and the noses pointed up like a mortar. The next shells fell in close. These were fragmenting shells that, upon exploding, sent bits of metal flying in all directions. The shells were causing panic in the camp. Those who did run were hit by the flying metal. Joseph told his three wards to stay in the dugout. He would try to get to White Bird and Looking Glass, he told them.

Within a few minutes a shell burst close to the dugout where Wetatonmi was lying. She heard her horse whinny with pain and looked out to see him down. Henawit was upstream another thirty feet and had not been hit. Wetatonmi told Young Ollikut to stay in the dugout. Climbing out, Wetatonmi ran to Partner and knelt down beside him. The metal had hit him in the throat and he was losing blood rapidly. Next to Young Ollikut, she loved this horse with all her heart. It had been Ollikut's first gift to her and one she had grown to love and cherish. She could see him finding it hard to breathe and knew he would not last long. Laying her head on his neck, she petted his head as he lay dying. Within a moment the life was gone. Could her heart hurt any more? What was she to endure? She knew that she could not live if anything were to happen to her son. She jumped up to start back to the dugout when she heard a loud bang close to her. She felt warm and light. She could see her husband, Ollikut, reaching his hand out to her. With one floating motion, she took it and was gone from the world of tears and trouble.

Chapter 24

SOME WILL GO

Joseph found White Bird easily, and now White Bird and he were searching for Looking Glass. As they approached his location, they could see some Indian riders coming up fast. They ducked down in the next wash just as Looking Glass jumped up and hollered, "See, it is Sitting Bull. He has come to help us escape." He no more finished his words than a shot rang out. Looking Glass spun around from the blow of a bullet in his forehead. He was dead.

There were no Sioux coming to help but rather more Cheyenne that he had mistaken for Sioux. Looking Glass was the last Nez Perce killed by the soldiers or their scouts for Howard sent word to Joseph that he wanted to parley.

The parley was set up and once Howard had Joseph in his camp, he was made a prisoner. White Bird then captured Lieutenant Jerome and Howard was forced to make a trade.

As soon as Joseph returned, he told White Bird of the terms of the surrender. White Bird, not willing to surrender, told Joseph that not all could get away, but that he and some of his people were going to try. Young Ollikut heard this and asked Joseph to let him go with White Bird. He said he knew his father would have taken him north if he were here. Joseph's own daughter asked if she might accompany Young Ollikut. His mother had comforted her when she lost her mother and now she wanted to watch over him as repayment for this kindness. Joseph did not like the idea, but White Bird said he had word that there was a chance that help was on its way. If Joseph could only stall for a while.

Joseph returned to Howard and agreed to surrender. He said, "I am tired of fighting. Our chiefs are killed. Looking Glass is dead. Toohulhulsote is dead. The old men are all dead. It is the young men who say yes or no. My brother who led the warriors is dead. It is cold and we have no blankets.

The little children are freezing to death. My people, some of them, have run away to the hills and have no blankets, no food. No one knows where they are, perhaps freezing to death. I want to have time to look for my children and see how many of them I can find. Maybe I shall find them among the dead. Hear me, my chiefs. I am tired, my heart is sick and sad. From where the sun now stands I will fight no more forever."

That night of October 5, 1877, there were fires and the soldiers gave the Nez Perce blankets and food. Over one hundred rifles were turned over to the soldiers. With this, Howard knew that he had won. He was in a good mood. The soldiers were relieved that there would be no more shooting. They had lost too many friends over the last four months.

Crazy Horse had not completely forgotten about the Nez Perce. Before he was captured, he had gathered 200 horses in a big meadow on the Missouri for the Nez Perce. With his capture, the horses had just roamed the small confines of the natural corral bordered by the river. When Looking Glass's two runners finally reached the Sioux Chief's homeland they discovered what had happened to Crazy Horse and were very disappointed that there would be no help or horses.

Before the day had passed, a young girl in her late teens came to the scouts. She said she was Twilight, the daughter of Chief Crazy Horse, and that she and her grandfather, Crowfoot, could take them to the horses Crazy Horse had collected for them. This was good news for the scouts so off the four of them rode.

A few nights later they approached the Bear Paw area with the horses from the north. A group of Cheyenne attacked the herd, but Crowfoot had put the horses on a hard run and all but thirty got through to White Bird.

Being as quiet as he could, White Bird gathered together all those who wanted to go with him and packed as much food and blankets as he could carry.

Young Ollikut and Running Spring were ready too. Henawit had been caught and was ready for the ride north. Young Ollikut would not leave without him. He knew that someday he too would have a fine horse herd like his father's and Henawit would be the sire of his fine spotted horses.

EPILOGUE

Young Ollikut and Running Spring did accompany White Bird to Canada. Sitting Bull's people sent guides to help them through the Assiniboine country, and once in Canada they were safe.

Joseph stayed behind with over 400 others who could not leave or would not. They were taken to Fort Keogh by Miles, then later to prison in Fort Leavenworth, Kansas. Years later Joseph was to meet with two different Presidents and petition them to return his people to the Wallowa. In 1899, twenty-two years after the surrender, Joseph and about 150 of his people that had been held in Oklahoma were returned to the Lapwai Valley.

With the gold Young Ollikut found in his father's belongings, he later bought horses and developed a horse herd in Canada. Selling most of them in 1902, he and his wife, accompanied by Joseph's daughter and family, departed for the Wallowa. They stopped at Lapwai to visit Joseph, and then Young Ollikut and his wife went on to the Wallowa where they bought out a settler and once again turned spotted Nez Perce horses loose to run in the Wallowa meadows.

Joseph died on the reservation in 1904 of a broken heart. He was just past sixty years old.

Ollikut had led his people on a retreat over one thousand miles in four months. He is remembered vaguely for his magnificent maneuvering, most of which was attributed to

Joseph by Howard and the newspaper articles at that time.

In 1936, a group of whites in the Moscow, Idaho, area started a movement to re-establish the spotted horses in the tri-state area.

After capturing the Nez Perce, Howard confiscated all the Indian ponies that were left. They were put up for sale. Farmers and ranchers purchased most of them. These fine horses were bred to draft horses and all kinds of inferior saddle horses. The Nez Perce horse was almost bred out of existence.

From 1936 to the seventies, the horses with recognizable spotted horse markings were selectively bred to bring back the genes of the spirit horses. These horses were then bred to top quality Arabians, Quarter Horses and some Thoroughbred horses.

Today we have the Appaloosa horse which exhibits the color of the Nez Perce spotted horse but still does not have the spirit of the horse that died at Bear Paw with Ollikut. Even Henawit left his great spirit in the draw with his friend.

Now, an Appaloosa is a special horse,
The Nez Perce developed without remorse.
They bred the finest and cut the rest.
So the offspring would be the very best.

The Nez Perce selected for special traits.
Not just any two Appys could be mates.
They had to have speed and endurance too.
The ones that didn't were sold to the Sioux.

The Appy was the wealth of Joseph's band.
So every horse wore an earmark brand.
The number of horses really didn't matter.
For on the grass they all grew fatter.

The Appy flourished for a hundred years.
Then came the white man, bringing heartache and tears.
In eighteen seventy-seven the order was made.
It commanded the Nez Perce to lay down the blade.

They were to be in Lapwai by June.
From now, that gave them one moon.
With the help of each rider, herds were collected.
Joseph felt their ownership would be protected.

The Snake ran high with the melting snow.
The horses must cross, they had to go.
Running the herd hard for the water,

The leaders went in with hardly a falter.

The mares and colts brought up the rear,
And every mother was filled with fear.
The colts had no training against such a foe,
They all lost their lives, not one it let go.

The people were safe on the opposite bank,
With the Appy and Great Spirit to thank.
But the Snake had swallowed nine hundred horses more.
The Nez Perce were sick, but the burden they bore.

There was no excuse for such ruthless orders.
Yet, they'd come from General Howard's quarters.
Now, the young braves were angry over such a fate,
Killing some whites, they vented their hate.

The Nez Perce war was thus started,
With the old and the wise broken hearted.
They knew that their numbers were small,
Before it was over many would fall.

If they were to fight there were too few,
Even though with time the numbers grew.
If they were to die there were too many,
For they wanted not to part with any.

With all their family belongings to carry,
They hastened away, for they must not tarry.
To leave the Wallowa, the land of their birth,
Was the hardest of all, for this was their earth.

The Appys proved worthy of their owners' pride.
They carried the Nez Perce on the long long ride.
Outrunning Howard, they crossed the river,
Then headed North, still in a shiver.

After five battles over sixteen hundred mils,
The army had its defeats recorded in the files.
The final battle had not yet been fought,
But at Bear Paw the Nez Perce were caught.

Colonel Miles charged with six hundred men.
The camp was smashed, recorded one pen.
More Nez Perce were killed in that one charge,
Than the rest of the time they had been at large.

The horses were scattered all over the hill.
With no means of escape, the Nez Perce must kill.
Then came the cannon that poured in the shell.
Death was all over from the look and the smell.

Joseph surrendered to save his small group.
The soldiers rode around them making a loop.
Before it was closed a few had fled,
North to freedom, by White Bird they were led.

The horses were promised returned to the tribe,
But instead they were sold for gold as a bribe.
Was this the end of the Appaloosa horse?
A breed such as this would not die, of course.

The Appy now made an excellent ranch mount,
But the number existing you could easily count.
Because of his qualities, the number grew.
A breed was restored, and a history too.

The Appaloosa Horse Club formed in Thirty-eight,
By owners who thought this breed real great.
Because of the crisis of World War II,
The horses and breeders still numbered few.

The breed today is growing so fast,
Other breeds it has even surpassed.
If Chief Joseph could see the Appy today,
"What a marvelous horse," he'd surely say.

"Mac"

REFERENCES

United States Government Documents and Publications. <u>Hear Me My Chiefs! Nez Perce Legend and History</u> by L.V. McWhorter. September 1952.

McWorter, L.V. <u>Yellow Wolf: His Own Story</u>. 2nd ed. March 1948.

Wilfong, Cheryl. <u>Following the Nez Perce Trail: A Guide to the Nee-Me-Poo National Historic Trail with Eyewitness Accounts</u>. 1990.

ABOUT THE AUTHOR

J'Wayne "Mac" McArthur is the retired Horsemanship Program Director at Utah State University in Logan, Utah. He taught horsemanship, colt breaking, horse judging, packing, roping, shoeing, and cowboy crafts.

While working for the U.S. Department of Agriculture, Economic Research Service after graduate school, Mac published research on many of the western states at USDA Washington, D.C. Upon joining the faculty at Utah State University, he continued publishing at that institution as well as New Mexico State University and University of Utah.

Mac has published many articles in national horse magazines including the Western Horseman, Quarter Horse Journal, Hoofs and Horns and The Appaloosa News. He has written weekly horse columns in the Herald Journal in Logan, Utah and the The Post Register in Idaho Falls, Idaho. He had columns in The Farmer Stockman magazine in Utah, Idaho, Washington, Oregon, Montana, and Nevada, as well as The Grainews magazine in Winnepeg, Canada for a number of years.

In 1990, Mac was named "Teacher of the Year" at Utah State University. At the age of 73, Mac was inducted into the 2009 Salmon Select Sale Hall of Fame in Salmon, Idaho as All-Time Champion and presented a beautiful Montana Silversmith buckle in recognition for buying the most horses over the years and selling top priced horses at the sale. Mac has owned over 1,000 head of horses and produced his own Broke Horse Sale for 13 years prior to retiring.

Training For Western Horse and Rider. *A 343 page guide to owning, riding and training the western horse with over 300 photographs and drawings. 6th Edition.*

The Cowboy Life in Short Stories and Poems. *A 126 page story and poem book to make you laugh and cry. 3rd Edition.*

The Friendly Beast, The First Domestication of the Horse. *A 43 page children's book about the domestication of the horse in Persia 5000 years ago.*

Two Trails, One Great Adventure. *A 61 page story for pet lovers.*

Spokane, 1889 Kentucky Derby Winner from Montana. *A 118 page book about a Montana horse that won the Kentucky Derby and set a race track speed record.*

Lonesome Cowboy. *A novel about the loneliness of a cowboy's life.*